GUIDE

Facebook®

Second Edition

by Mikal E. Belicove and Joe Kraynak

ALPHA

A member of Penguin Group (USA) Inc.

ALPHA BOOKS

Published by the Penguin Group

Penguin Group (USA) Inc., 375 Hudson Street, New York, New York 10014, USA

Penguin Group (Canada), 90 Eglinton Avenue East, Suite 700, Toronto, Ontario M4P 2Y3, Canada (a division of Pearson Penguin Canada Inc.)

Penguin Books Ltd., 80 Strand, London WC2R 0RL, England

Penguin Ireland, 25 St. Stephen's Green, Dublin 2, Ireland (a division of Penguin Books Ltd.)

Penguin Group (Australia), 250 Camberwell Road, Camberwell, Victoria 3124, Australia (a division of Pearson Australia Group Pty. Ltd.)

Penguin Books India Pvt. Ltd., 11 Community Centre, Panchsheel Park, New Delhi—110 017, India

Penguin Group (NZ), 67 Apollo Drive, Rosedale, North Shore, Auckland 1311, New Zealand (a division of Pearson New Zealand Ltd.)

Penguin Books (South Africa) (Pty.) Ltd., 24 Sturdee Avenue, Rosebank, Johannesburg 2196, South Africa

Penguin Books Ltd., Registered Offices: 80 Strand, London WC2R 0RL, England

Copyright © 2011 by Mikal E. Belicove and Joe Kraynak

International Standard Book Number: 978-1-61564-118-5
Library of Congress Catalog Card Number: 2011904912

13   12   11   8   7   6   5   4   3   2   1

Interpretation of the printing code: The rightmost number of the first series of numbers is the year of the book's printing; the rightmost number of the second series of numbers is the number of the book's printing. For example, a printing code of 11-1 shows that the first printing occurred in 2011.

Printed in the United States of America

Note: This publication contains the opinions and ideas of its authors. It is intended to provide helpful and informative material on the subject matter covered. It is sold with the understanding that the authors and publisher are not engaged in rendering professional services in the book. If the reader requires personal assistance or advice, a competent professional should be consulted.

The authors and publisher specifically disclaim any responsibility for any liability, loss, or risk, personal or otherwise, which is incurred as a consequence, directly or indirectly, of the use and application of any of the contents of this book.

Most Alpha books are available at special quantity discounts for bulk purchases for sales promotions, premiums, fund-raising, or educational use. Special books, or book excerpts, can also be created to fit specific needs.

For details, write: Special Markets, Alpha Books, 375 Hudson Street, New York, NY 10014.

Publisher: *Marie Butler-Knight*
Associate Publisher/Acquiring Editor: *Mike Sanders*
Executive Managing Editor: *Billy Fields*
Development Editor/Copy Editor: *Jennifer Moore*

Senior Production Editor: *Kayla Dugger*
Cover Designer: *Rebecca Batchelor*
Book Designers: *William Thomas, Rebecca Batchelor*
Indexer: *Angie Martin*
Layout: *Brian Massey*
Senior Proofreader: *Laura Caddell*

From Mikal: *To my 76-year-old mother, Glenda Belicove, who taught me everything I ever needed to know about living an authentic life, as well as a few things about using Facebook!*

From Joe: *To Facebook users worldwide, who make Facebook the most intriguing digital hangout on the planet.*

Contents

Part 1:   **Mastering Facebook Basics 1**

1   **Meeting Facebook Face to Face 3**

What Is Facebook, Anyway? 3

Putting Your Face on Facebook 5

   Finding Friends and Entering Your Info 6

   Finding Friends Using Your E-Mail Address Book 6

   Entering School and Workplace Information 7

   Upload a Digital Photo of Yourself 8

   Completing the Sign Up Process 10

   Logging In and Logging Out 11

In Your Face with the Interface 11

   Scooting Up to the Top Menu 12

   Catching Up on Your News Feed 14

   Checking Out the Publisher 14

   Exploring the Left Menu 14

   Exploring the Column on the Right 15

Adjusting Your Account Settings 15

Following Facebook Rules and Etiquette 17

   Rules and Regulations 17

   Etiquette 18

Help! Navigating Facebook's Help System 19

Quitting Facebook 20

   Deactivating Your Account 20

   Deleting Your Account 21

2   **Protecting Your Privacy and Profile 23**

Setting Your Privacy Preferences 23

   Connecting on Facebook 25

   Sharing on Facebook 26

   Apps and Websites Privacy 28

   Blocking Annoying Individuals 31

Defending Yourself from Hackers and Phishers 32

   Keeping Hackers from Hijacking Your Account 33

   Dodging Phishing Schemes 34

   Preventing and Stopping Spam 35

   Reporting Scams and Schemes to Facebook 36

   A Word to Parents … 36

3   Fleshing Out Your Personal Profile 39

Accessing Your Profile to Adjust It 39

Changing Your Profile Photo.. 40

Uploading a Digital Photo 41

Snapping a Photo with Your Webcam................................ 42

Selecting a Picture for Your Profile.................................. 44

Clipping Your Thumbnail... 44

Hiding and Unhiding the Photos in the Photostream............45

Editing Information About Yourself.................................. 46

Basic Information 46

Featured People.. 47

Education and Work.. 48

Personal Information 48

Contact Information 49

**4   Connecting with Friends, Family,
       and Classmates 51**

Knowing What It Means to Be a Friend 51

Sharing Walls and News Feeds 52

Sharing Photo Albums 52

Sharing Information... 53

Digging Up People You Know 53

Searching for an Individual by Name or E-Mail 54

Searching for People in Your E-Mail Address Book 54

Finding Friends, Classmates, and Co-Workers 56

Seeing Who Your Friends Are 58

Befriending and De-Friending 58

Sending a Friend Request 59

Responding to a Friend Request...59

Dumping a Friend.. 60

Creating and Managing Friend Lists 61

Expanding Your Reach with Networks 63

Introducing Your Friends 65

5   Hitting the Wall ... and Your News Feed 67

Homing In on Your News Feed 68

Checking Out Your Wall... 70

Heading to Your Wall 70

Bumping Into a Friend's Wall 71

Posting to Your Wall or News Feed 72

  Posting a Question *73*

  Attaching a Photo *74*

  Attaching a Video *76*

  Inserting a Link *76*

  Adding Other Stuff 77

Responding to a Friend's Post 77

  Posting a Comment 78

  Voting Your Approval 78

  Hiding a Friend's Status Updates 79

Posting to a Friend's Wall 80

  Connecting One-on-One via a Friendship Page 80

  Wishing a Friend a Happy Birthday 82

  Poking a Friend 82

Liking and Sharing Stuff 83

**6   Communicating with
      Facebook Messaging** **87**

Activating E-Mail, Texting, and Chat 87

Accessing Messages 88

  Reading and Replying to New Messages 89

  Adding Someone to the Conversation 90

  Leaving the Conversation *91*

  Forwarding a Message *91*

  Searching for Messages *91*

  Flagging Messages as Unread 92

  Archiving or Deleting a Message 93

  Reporting Spam *93*

Outgoing! Sending Messages 93

  Sending a New Message to a Facebook Member 94

  Sending a Message to an Address Outside Facebook *95*

  Mass Mailing to Multiple Recipients *95*

Taking Notice of Notifications 96

Part 2: Getting More Involved with Facebook **99**

7   Uploading and Sharing Photos **101**

Looking at Photos 101

Preparing Photos for Uploading 103

  Editing Your Photos: Quality Counts *103*

  Organizing Photos into Folders *104*

Uploading Photos 104
Uploading Photos to a New Album *105*
Uploading Photos to an Existing Album *107*
Editing Your Photos and Albums 107
Working on Individual Photos *108*
Tagging Photos *109*
Rearranging Photos in Your Album *111*
Managing Your Photos with
  Third-Party Applications 112
Linking to Picasa *113*
Linking to Flickr *114*

8   Uploading and Sharing Video Footage 117
Viewing Other People's Video Clips 117
Watching a Video Clip *118*
Commenting on a Video Clip *119*
Tagging a Video Clip *119*
Watching Videos in Which You've Been Tagged *120*
Recording and Uploading Video Footage 121
Taking Note of Facebook's Video Guidelines *121*
Accessing the Video Page *122*
Uploading a Video Clip from Your Computer *123*
Recording Video Using Your Webcam *124*
Editing Video Information 125
Embedding a Video 126
Sending a Video Message via E-Mail 127

9   Getting Organized with Groups 129
Understanding Groups: Open, Closed, and Secret 129
Exploring Existing Groups 130
Searching for a Group *130*
Finding Groups Through Your Friends *131*
Checking Out a Group *132*
Getting Involved in a Group 133
Joining a Group *133*
Leaving a Group *133*
Conversing in Groups 133
Unsubscribing from a Conversation *135*

Creating Your Own Group................................135

   Creating a Group E-Mail Address........................136

   Adding Friends to the Group.............................137

   Making Someone Else an Administrator................137

   Removing Group Members................................137

Sharing Photos Within the Group 138

Creating an Event...138

Chatting with the Group...................................139

Collaborating on a Group Document........................ 140

10   Chatting with Friends in Real Time............. 143

Let's Chat!.. 144

   Viewing and Deleting Your Chat History........................145

   Going Offline or Back Online.............................146

Engaging in a Video Call 147

Chatting in a Group..149

Setting Your Chat Options................................150

   Pop-Out Chat.. 151

   Play Sound for New Messages.............................152

   Keep Online Friends Window Open....................152

   Show Only Names in Online Friends.................153

Setting Friend List Options 153

   Display or Hide a Friend List............................153

   Go Offline or Online with a Group of Friends.................154

   Create a New Friend List................................154

11   Partay! Tracking and Announcing Events.....157

Accessing and Navigating the Events App 158

Checking Scheduled Events 158

   Poking Around for Events................................159

   Searching and Browsing Events.........................160

   RSVP-ing an Event You Plan to Attend..................161

Announcing Your Own Special Event.....................162

   Creating an Event.......................................163

   Keeping Your Guests in the Loop......................165

12   Taking Notes ... and Sharing Them............. 169

What Are Notes Exactly?....................................169

Entering the Notes Zone...................................170

   Perusing Your Friends' Notes............................171

   Commenting on Existing Notes........................172

Liking a Friend's Note..*172*
Sharing a Friend's Note..*172*
Posting a New Note 173
Reviewing Your Notes..*175*
Finding Out Who's Talking About You............................*175*
Feeding Blog Posts into Notes 176

Part 3: Harnessing the Power of Facebook Apps.....179

13   Exploring More Facebook Apps 181
Grasping the Basics of Facebook Apps 181
Digging Up More Apps..*182*
Evaluating and Authorizing Apps *184*
Addressing Security Concerns *186*
Responding to and Sending App Requests.......................187
Responding to an App Request...*187*
Inviting Your Friends to Use an Application *188*
Editing and Removing Applications 189

**14   Playing Games with Friends
        and Strangers 191**
Oh, the Games People Play!..191
Finding Games on Facebook...194
Let's Play Already!..195
Launching a Game *196*
Encouraging Your Friends to Play *197*
Making New Friends Through Games *198*
Responding to a Friend's Request to Play..........................*198*

15   Facebooking with Your Mobile Phone 201
Accessing Facebook with a Smartphone App 202
Setting Up Facebook Mobile... 202
Texting to Facebook.. 204
Posting Status Updates *205*
Texting Facebook Commands *205*
Uploading Photos and Videos from Your Phone 207
Taking Facebook Mobile Web on the Road.................... 208

Checking in with Facebook Places.....................209
    Getting Started *210*
    Checking In.......................*210*
    Adjusting Your Places Privacy Settings.......................*211*
Taking Advantage of Check-In Deals.....................211
    Finding Check-In Deals..........................*212*
    Sharing Deals with Your Friends.......................*213*

Part 4:   Getting Down to Business on Facebook.......215

16   **Doing Business in a Social Setting.................217**
The Business Case for Facebook...........................217
Tapping the Power of Facebook Advertising....................219
    Launching a Facebook Page.............................*219*
    Cross-Promoting Facebook on Your Blog or Website *220*
    Posting Ads on Facebook.............................*221*
    Going Viral with Facebook for Websites..........................*221*
    Tapping the Power of Places and Deals...........................*222*
Establishing a Following with Groups 222
Engaging Members with Facebook Applications..............223
Do's and Don'ts of Doing Business on Facebook..............224

17   **Launching and Managing a
Business Page.....................................227**
The Business Case for a Page...........................228
Crafting and Customizing Your Page...............................228
    Laying the Groundwork.......................*229*
    Creating Your Page..........................*230*
    Getting Back to Your Page.............................*232*
    Adjusting Your Page Settings.............................*233*
    Hiding or Deleting Pages.............................*236*
Adding Compelling Content to Your Page 236
    Expanding Content with Other Facebook Apps..................*238*
    Accessorizing Your Page with Third-Party Apps *238*
    Feeding Your Blog to Your Facebook Business Page...........*238*
Building and Maintaining Your Fan Base 240
Tracking Page Effectiveness with Page Insights..............241

18   Mastering the Soft Sell with Social Ads...... 245

Weighing the Pros and Cons of Facebook Ads 245

  Potential Benefits 246

  Potential Drawbacks 247

Laying the Groundwork 248

  Brushing Up on Facebook Ads Rules and Regulations 248

  Setting a Measurable Goal 249

  Targeting a Demographic and Locale 250

  Listing a Few Keywords 250

  Settling on a Call to Action 250

  Composing an Effective Message 251

  Finding Just the Right Picture 251

Launching Your Advertising Campaign 252

  Creating Your Ad 252

  Targeting Your Demographic 253

  Choosing a Campaign, Pricing, and Scheduling 254

  Reviewing and Approving Your Ad 255

  Monitoring and Fine-Tuning Your Campaign 256

19   Marketing with Places and Deals...................259

Claiming Your Place 259

  Check for Your Place 260

  Add a Place 260

  Claim Your Place 261

  Merging Your Place and Page 261

Offering Check-In Deals 262

  Recognizing the Four Types of Check-In Deals 263

  Let's Make a Deal 263

  Promoting Your Check-In Deals 264

  Offering Other Deals on Facebook 265

Appendixes

Glossary 267

Index 271

Introduction

In the days B.C. (Before Computers), losing touch with friends and family was a part of life. You'd graduate and all your school chums would wander off in different directions. You'd leave your job and lose valuable contacts. Aunts, uncles, and cousins would seem to fall off the face of the earth. Even keeping in touch with siblings hundreds or thousands of miles away was a challenge.

Facebook, with the help of computers and the Internet, has reversed that trend. Not only does it enable you to stay in touch with people, but it also facilitates the process of tracking down people you lost touch with years or decades ago. Facebook also provides numerous ways for you to engage and interact with all these folks daily—by sharing status updates, photos, and videos; posting links to favorite web pages or blogs; chatting; messaging; playing games; planning events; gathering in groups; and so on. And if you're in business (big or small), Facebook provides several valuable tools to keep in touch with customers and clients right where many of them like to hang out most.

Perhaps best of all, Facebook is free, and all you need to get started is a computer with an Internet connection and a desire to connect with others. If you're concerned about privacy, you'll be relieved to know that Facebook gives you complete control over whom you choose to "friend" and the information you choose to share.

If you're concerned that you don't know where to start, that's where we come in. In this book, we provide everything you need to know to get started on Facebook; track down friends, family members, colleagues, former classmates, and others; promote your business or yourself; and tap the full potential of Facebook.

Disclaimer: Facebook is in a constant state of change as its developers introduce new features and adjust the ways that Facebook members interact with the service and with one another. During the writing of the book, we checked everything, step by step, not once, not twice, but three times to verify its accuracy prior to publication, but we're 99.99 percent sure that by the time you read this, something will have changed. We tried to make the instructions specific enough to be useful and general enough to cover minor changes, but you may need to consult Facebook's Help system for details and changes. We show you how in Chapter 1.

What You Learn in This Book

You don't have to read this book from cover to cover (although you might miss some succulent tidbits if you skip around). If you haven't even signed up with Facebook, start with Chapter 1 to register, log in, and take a brief tour of Facebook's core features. If you're concerned about privacy issues, skip to Chapter 2, where we show you how to adjust your privacy settings. To track down people and invite them to be your Facebook friends, head to Chapter 4. Chapter 7 shows you how to share photos, one of Facebook's most popular features.

As for the rest of the chapters, each covers a specific Facebook feature. To provide some structure for this hodgepodge of features, we've grouped the chapters into the following four parts and tacked on a glossary at the end:

Part 1, Mastering Facebook Basics, shows you how to sign up, sign in, add a photo and information to your Facebook Profile, tweak the privacy settings to your comfort level, track down friends and family and add them as Facebook friends, keep in touch with friends via Walls and News Feeds, and contact people in private via the Message feature (e-mail plus). We also show you how to leave Facebook with or without leaving personal information behind.

Part 2, Getting More Involved with Facebook, ramps you up to some more advanced Facebook features, including photo sharing, video sharing, Groups, Chat, Events, and Notes (sort of like blogging). After logging on and figuring out what the Wall and News Feed are all about, these are the features you tackle next.

Part 3, Harnessing the Power of Facebook Apps, introduces you to some higher-level applications (or apps, for short) designed to enhance the Facebook experience. Here, you learn how to access core Facebook apps, explore Facebook's robust collection of third-party apps, and use the Mobile app to access Facebook from your smartphone.

Part 4, Getting Down to Business on Facebook, helps you unleash the power of social-media marketing on Facebook. After a brief chapter on how you can use Facebook to promote yourself, your business, or your products and services, we show you how to create and promote a business-based Facebook Page (sometimes called a fan page); use Facebook ads to drive traffic to your website, blog, or page; strengthen your brand; list yourself in Facebook Places; and offer Facebook members special deals.

Conventions Used in This Book

We use several conventions in this book to make it easier to understand. For example, when you need to type something, it appears **bold**.

Likewise, if we tell you to select or click a command, the command appears **bold**. This enables you to quickly scan a series of steps without having to wade through all the text.

Extras

A plethora of sidebars offer additional information about what you've just read. Here's what to look for:

FRIEND-LY ADVICE

During our days on Facebook, we discovered easier, faster, and better ways to perform certain tasks and maximize the power of specific features. Here, we share these tips with you.

WHOA!

Before you click that button, skim the page for one of these sidebars, each of which offers a precautionary note. Chances are, we've made the mistake ourselves, so let us tell you how to avoid the same blunder.

> **POKE**
>
> On Facebook, you can poke your Facebook friends when they're online to let them know you're thinking about them. As you might imagine, this can get annoying if someone overdoes it. We include pokes throughout the book to cue you in on lesser-known features of Facebook. Hopefully, you'll find our pokes more compelling than most.

Acknowledgments

Several people contributed to building and perfecting this book. We owe special thanks to Tom Stevens and Mike Sanders for choosing us to author this book and for handling the assorted details to get it in gear. Thanks to Jennifer Moore for guiding the content, keeping it focused on new users, ferreting out all our typos, and fine-tuning our sentences. Kayla Dugger deserves a free trip to Tahiti for shepherding the manuscript (and art) through production. The Alpha Books production team merits a round of applause for transforming a collection of electronic files into such an attractive book.

Finally, we'd be remiss if we failed to thank the dozen or so Facebook members—our friends, both on and off Facebook—who served as guinea pigs and allowed us to capture their Facebook activity in the screen shots you see throughout this book. To Adam W. Chase, Al Rotches, Amy McCloskey Tobin, Andy Marker, BlackPast.org, Brighton Feed & Saddlery, Chris Ochs, Debra Oakland, Ford Reese Church, Glenda Belicove, Jay Muntz, Jennifer St. James, Jerry Chrisman, Michael McKenzie, Nirvana Grille, Paul Ford, Peter Leibfred, R. Scott Torgan, Sam Williams, Scott D. Slater, Stuart Lisonbee, Susan Cherones, and Tanya Payne, thank you very much; this book wouldn't have been possible without your witty status updates, photos, and more.

Trademarks

Mastering Facebook Basics

Everyone on Facebook has had a first encounter with it—staring at the screen, bewildered as to what's going on, and uncertain on how to proceed. It's sort of like stepping foot in a foreign country, where you're unsure of the customs and can't even figure out how to plug in your hair dryer without turning it into toast.

In this part, we re-create the first-encounter experience without the fear and bewilderment. We show you how to sign up, sign in, flesh out your Profile, upload a Profile photo, protect your personal information, find people, make friends, and interact with others via Walls and News Feeds. In other words, we bring you up to speed on the basics.

Meeting Facebook Face to Face

In This Chapter

- Finding out what this Facebook thing is all about
- Getting your face on Facebook
- Making your way around
- Brushing up on Facebook etiquette
- Getting help

At your next party or family get-together, somebody is sure to mention Facebook. When they do, ask, "What's Facebook?" The room is likely to fall silent (except for a few scattered giggles), and then everyone in the room who's had any experience with Facebook will start to trip over one another trying to explain it to you.

Everyone seems to be on Facebook … except you. Well, that's about to change. It's high time to lose your Facebook virginity and join the rest of your friends and family in the twenty-first century. In this chapter, we introduce you to Facebook, show you how to register and log in, and then take you on a nickel tour to get you up to speed on the basics.

What Is Facebook, Anyway?

Facebook is a free online social-networking venue where friends, family, colleagues, and acquaintances can mingle, get to know one another better, and expand their social circles.

After you register and log in to Facebook, as explained in the following section, you can invite people you know to join you on Facebook and become your friend. Any friends already on Facebook can invite you to become their Facebook friend, too. (We cover the whole making friends thing in Chapter 4.)

Once you have a Facebook friend or two, you can begin exchanging notes by posting status updates to your News Feed. A status update essentially tells your Facebook friends what you're doing, thinking, or feeling. Your News Feed is a running record of status updates and more posted by you and your friends. The "and more" can include photos and video clips that you and your friends post, links to interesting stuff on the web, notes you create to post something longer than a status update, results of quizzes and polls you participate in, and more.

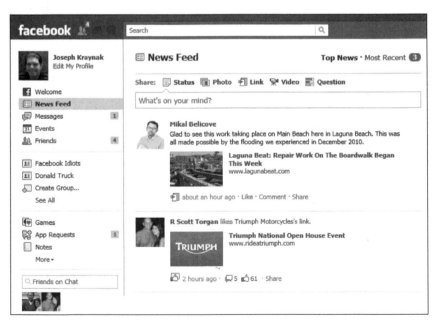

Your News Feed keeps you in touch with your friends.

That's Facebook in a nutshell, but you can do much more than simply swap messages with your buddies. Following are some of the more popular activities you may want to engage in:

- Dig up old friends and classmates.

- Track down family members who've wandered from the fold.

- Expand your social and professional circles by connecting with friends of friends and current and former co-workers.

- Share photos, videos, and links to interesting web pages.

- Recommend books, movies, and music.

- Exchange birthday wishes and gifts.

- Play games.

- Spread the word about political causes and charities.

- Invite guests to parties and other get-togethers and keep track of who's planning to attend.

- Text and audio/video chat with your friends online ... assuming they're online when you are.

- Buy and sell stuff, find a job, and market yourself or your business.

POKE

Facebook is in a perpetual process of evolution. By the time you read this, additional features may be available.

Putting Your Face on Facebook

Before you can join the revelry, you have to put your face (and name) on Facebook by registering. This entails entering your e-mail address, choosing a password, and providing some basic information about yourself, including your name, sex, and birthday. To register, follow these steps:

1. Fire up your web browser and head to www.facebook.com.

2. Complete the Sign Up form. It provides the instruction you need.

3.   Click **Sign Up**. Facebook might display a security check screen prompting you to type a string of characters shown on the screen.

4.   If a security check appears, type the text that appears as directed, click **Sign Up**, and proceed to the following section.

*Complete the form and click **Sign Up**.*

Finding Friends and Entering Your Info

After you register, Facebook steps you through the process of finding friends, entering basic information like schools you've attended and places you've worked, and uploading a digital photo of yourself. All of these steps are optional, so you can safely click **Skip** at each step and do all this later at your leisure. If you'd rather do it now, proceed to the following section.

Finding Friends Using Your E-Mail Address Book

The first order of business is to find some friends. If the e-mail address you used to sign on to Facebook is web-based, like Gmail

(Google e-mail), and your e-mail account has an address book with contacts listed in it, Facebook can extract e-mail addresses from your address book and use them to locate any Facebook members who log in using any of those addresses.

Don't worry, Facebook won't send out friend invitations to everyone in your address book without your permission. You'll have a chance to select the people you want to invite. To find potential friends now, enter the password associated with your e-mail account, click **Find Friends**, and follow instructions. If you don't know your e-mail password, you will be unable to use this feature. Try contacting your e-mail service provider to have your password reset. For more about finding friends, see Chapter 4.

Facebook can find friends for you.

Entering School and Workplace Information

In Step 2 you're asked to enter information about your high school, college, and one place you've worked. Facebook uses this information to search for even more people you may know—people who graduated from the same high school or college the same year you did or who worked at the same company.

Enter any or all of the requested information and click **Save & Continue** or just click **Skip**.

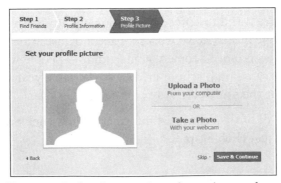

Enter school and workplace information to enlist Facebook's assistance in tracking down classmates and co-workers.

If you choose **Save & Continue**, Facebook displays a selection of Facebook members it has identified as people with whom you may have graduated or worked. You can select any or all of these people and then click **Save & Continue** to invite them to be your friends. Facebook displays people you may know based on the Profile information you've entered so far. Click **Add as friend** next to each person you want to request to be a friend and click **Save & Continue**, or click **Skip** to skip this step.

Facebook displays the third step in getting started: uploading a photo of yourself, as discussed next.

Upload a Digital Photo of Yourself

If you have a digital photo of yourself stored on your computer, or a webcam plugged into your computer so you can take a photo of yourself, you can add your mug shot, called a *Profile picture*, to your Profile. In Step 3 of getting started, click **Upload a Photo** or **Take a Photo**.

You can upload a photo or take a photo using a webcam.

If you click **Upload a Photo**, the Upload Your Profile Picture dialog box appears, prompting you to specify the photo file you want to use. Click **Browse**, use the resulting dialog box to select a digital photo of yourself stored on your computer, and click **Open**. Facebook uploads the photo and inserts it in your Profile.

If you click **Take a Photo**, the Take a Photo dialog box appears. If the Adobe Flash Player Settings dialog box appears, click **Allow** and then **Close**. Click the camera icon, say "Cheese" into your webcam, and wait three seconds for Facebook to snap your photo. If you like what you see, click **Save Picture**. If you don't like it, click **Cancel** and reshoot.

You can snap a picture of yourself using a webcam.

When you're happy with your Profile picture, click **Save & Continue**.

Completing the Sign Up Process

To complete the sign up process, check your Inbox for the e-mail address you used to sign up. You should have an e-mail message from Facebook with a link to click to confirm that this is, in fact, a valid e-mail address for an account you have access to. Click the link or the **Complete Sign-Up** button to validate with Facebook.

Facebook also logs you in and displays a screen with additional steps you can take at this time, including searching one of your e-mail accounts to find people you may already know on Facebook, fleshing out your Profile with additional information, activating your mobile phone, and controlling the information you share. It's a good idea to go through these steps now so Facebook doesn't keep bugging you about them, but you can skip them by clicking **Home** in the top menu (the dark blue bar).

To perform these steps later, Chapter 2 explains how to adjust your privacy settings to control the information you share on Facebook, Chapter 3 shows you how to flesh out your personal Profile, Chapter 4 explains how to find friends on Facebook, and Chapter 15 shows you how to activate your mobile phone.

You can step through the process of establishing yourself on Facebook.

Logging In and Logging Out

Now that you have a username (your e-mail address) and password, you can log in and out of Facebook whenever the spirit moves you. Just head to Facebook's Home page at www.facebook.com, type the e-mail address you used to register in the **Email** box, type your password in the **Password** box, and click **Login**. Facebook logs you in and displays your Home page, which features your News Feed and provides access to the rest of Facebook from one convenient location. To exit Facebook, click **Account > Logout** in the upper-right corner of the screen.

Enter your e-mail address and password to log on.

WHOA!

If someone else has access to your computer, log out when you're done on Facebook. Otherwise, someone can easily log in, read the discussions you're having with your friends, view your photos and videos, and post status updates pretending they're coming from you. They can even change your password, preventing *you* from logging in! Another option: When you're logging in, deselect the option **Keep me logged in** (if it's checked) before clicking the **Login** button. That way, Facebook logs you out automatically when you exit.

In Your Face with the Interface

When you log in, Facebook gets in your face with all the buttons, bars, links, icons, and menus you need to access everything. Facebook has done a nice job of organizing all this stuff, but the interface can seem a little overwhelming at first. Here, we highlight the main areas you need to focus on, then describe them in more detail in the sections that follow. If you don't see a screen with this stuff on it, click **Home** (in the top menu).

Core applications   Publisher   News Feed   Top menu

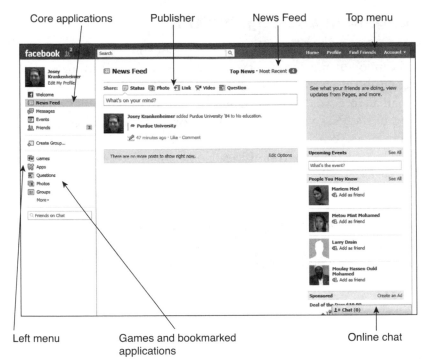

Left menu   Games and bookmarked   Online chat
                   applications

Facebook's interface.

Scooting Up to the Top Menu

The top menu (formerly known as "the blue bar") is Old Reliable. It appears at the top of the window no matter where you are or what you're doing on Facebook, providing quick access to the following features (from left to right on the bar):

- **Facebook:** Clicking the Facebook icon takes you Home—to the page that greets you when you sign on.

- **Friend Requests:** Click the **Friend Requests** icon, and a menu drops down displaying any Facebook members who are asking to be your friend. The menu also contains a Find Your Friends link you can click to search for your friends on Facebook. See Chapter 4 for more about friends.

- **Messages:** Click the **Messages** icon, and Facebook displays a list of any messages you received from other Facebook members. The menu also contains the Send a New Message

link you can click to compose and send a message to someone on Facebook. See Chapter 6 for more about Facebook's
Message (e-mail) feature.

- **Notifications:** Click the **Notifications** icon to view a list
  of your Facebook friends' current activities that pertain to
  you. Facebook notifies you whenever someone sends you a
  message, posts something on your Wall, or comments on
  something you commented on.

- **Search:** Click in the **Search** box, type a search word or
  phrase, and press **Enter** or **Return** on your computer key-
  board to search Facebook for people, places, things, or help
  with a particular feature.

- **Home:** Click **Home**, and Facebook takes you to your Home
  page, where you can view your News Feed.

- **Profile:** Click **Profile** to display your Profile page, where
  you can access your Wall, information about yourself, your
  photo albums, and other items of interest. In Chapter 3, you
  learn how to edit your Profile. In Chapter 5, you meet the
  Wall.

- **Find Friends:** Click **Find Friends**, and Facebook takes you
  to the "We'd like to help you find your friends" page, where
  you can search for people you know on Facebook and invite
  them to be your Facebook friends so you can communicate
  with one another. You can also invite people you know who
  aren't Facebook members, but they'll have to join Facebook
  before you can become Facebook friends.

- **Account:** Click **Account**, and a menu drops down providing access to several options: Edit Friends, Use Facebook as
  Page (see Chapter 17), Account Settings, Privacy Settings,
  Help Center, and Logout. Edit Friends takes you to a screen
  where you can search for and add more Facebook friends.
  We have details on Facebook Pages in Chapter 17 and talk
  more about the "Settings" options later in this chapter. The
  last two options are pretty obvious—you can get help or log
  out of Facebook.

Catching Up on Your News Feed

The News Feed is the core component of Facebook, providing you with a running account of just about everything you and your Facebook friends are up to and have agreed to share with one another. (In Chapter 2, you learn how to change your privacy settings if you want to share less.)

You can switch your News Feed to display Top News or Most Recent by clicking the desired option just above the News Feed. Top News displays a list of what Facebook deems are the most interesting posts from your Facebook friends. Most Recent displays all your friends' posts, starting with the most recent.

Checking Out the Publisher

At the top of your News Feed is your own personal Publisher. Whenever you want to post something to your News Feed, click in the Publisher's text box (the box containing "What's on your mind?"), type your message, and click **Share**. In addition to text messages, you can post photos, videos, links, or a question to poll your friends and see what they think. See Chapter 5 for a thorough explanation of the Publisher.

Exploring the Left Menu

The left menu (to the left of the News Feed) contains links for the most popular features on Facebook, including the following:

- **You:** At the top of the left menu is your Profile picture (assuming you added one), your name, and a link called "Edit My Profile." Click your photo or name, and Facebook displays your Profile page. See Chapter 3 for more about your Profile. Click **Edit My Profile** to change information you've entered about yourself.

- **Core features:** The next section down provides links to gain quick access to the four core Facebook features: News Feed, Messages, Events, and Friends. You'll find out more about all these features in later chapters.

- **Groups:** Below the core features is a Groups section that initially contains only one option: Create Group. As you join or create groups, links for them appear here.

- **Applications and Games:** This section contains links to Facebook's collection of applications and games, along with links to popular Facebook applications (apps for short), including Notes, Photos, Deals, and Questions.

- **Chat:** Below the Applications and Games section is a Go Online link you can click to make yourself available to chat with any of your Facebook friends. This also opens the Chat menu (lower-right corner of the screen), displaying the names of any of your friends who are online. You can click a friend's name to start chatting with them or initiate a video call. See Chapter 10 for more about Facebook's Chat feature. When you're online and want to go offline, click the **Chat** option (lower-right corner of the screen), mouse over **Options**, and click **Go offline**.

Exploring the Column on the Right

The column on the right contains a hodgepodge of items of varying importance, including upcoming events, people you may know, and sponsored ads or announcements.

Adjusting Your Account Settings

Facebook provides all sorts of ways to customize your experience, and it divides your options into two categories: Account Settings and Privacy Settings, which include a separate collection of settings for Apps and Websites. In Chapter 2, we tackle privacy issues and show you how to tweak your privacy settings to share more or less information in accordance with your personal preferences. In Chapter 13, you learn how to change your apps and websites settings. With those two out of the way, only account settings remain.

To change your account settings, click **Account** (in the top menu) and then **Account Settings**. Navigate the following tabs to enter your preferences.

- **Settings:** Most items on the Settings tab let you change information you entered when you registered with Facebook—your name, username, e-mail address, and password. You can also link your account to other accounts, including Google, Yahoo!, and myOpenID, so when you log in to those accounts, you're automatically logged in to Facebook; access your privacy settings; change account security settings; and even deactivate your account.

- **Networks:** On the Networks tab, you can join a network, change a region, and leave a network. For details on using networks to find friends, check out Chapter 4.

- **Notifications:** Whenever just about anything happens on Facebook that involves you, Facebook can send a notification to the e-mail address you used to register your account. You can use the options on the Notifications tab to enable or disable these e-mail notifications for certain actions and enable SMS (Short Message Service) options to be notified via your cell phone or smartphone. (You can always see your notifications by logging on to Facebook and clicking the **Notifications** icon near the left end of the top menu.)

- **Mobile:** The Mobile tab provides options to enable or disable Facebook for use with your cell phone or other smartphone. Enabling the mobile features allows Facebook to send notifications to your phone and allows you to post status updates, search for phone numbers, and upload photos and videos from your phone. For more about using Facebook with your cell phone or smartphone, check out Chapter 15.

- **Language:** If Facebook displays its options in a language you don't understand, you can click the **Language** tab and select a different language.

- **Payments:** Don't panic! Facebook is free. However, if you engage in business transactions, such as buying gifts for your friends or purchasing online advertising, you can click the **Payments** tab to enter payment preferences (Visa, MasterCard, and so on) and choose your preferred currency (dollar, euro, yen, and so on) for displaying prices and credit card charges.

- **Facebook Ads:** If you're concerned about your name or photo showing up in an advertisement on Facebook, click the **Facebook Ads** tab to learn more about what Facebook allows and prohibits in terms of advertisers using member information. This page includes links that you can click to view current ad settings and change the settings, if desired, to control how Facebook uses or may use your information now or in the future. For more about advertising on Facebook, check out Chapter 18.

FRIEND-LY ADVICE

If you're tired of being notified every time one of your friends sneezes on Facebook, head to the Notifications settings to make some adjustments.

Following Facebook Rules and Etiquette

To flourish as a social-networking service, Facebook must provide enough freedom to allow members to express themselves, find one another, and exchange information, but not so much freedom that members are subject to harassment or having their personal information published without their permission. As a result, Facebook has some rules for members to follow and etiquette guidelines to help members police their own behaviors.

Rules and Regulations

Facebook sets the rules that govern membership in its Terms of Service, which you can read in its entirety by scrolling down to the footer and clicking **Terms**. They basically boil down to the following do's and don'ts:

- Do provide accurate and current information in your Profile.

- Don't use Facebook to do anything illegal, immoral, or unethical.

- Do respect the rights of other members.

- Don't spam.

- Don't collect user information for marketing purposes without Facebook's permission.

- Don't do anything malicious to Facebook, including uploading viruses or unleashing denial-of-service attacks.

Etiquette

In the world of social networking, the rules of etiquette carry about as much weight as the Terms of Service. They not only protect others from being exposed to ill-mannered behavior, but they also protect members from the embarrassment that often follows from failing to act in accordance with a community's social norms. Following are several etiquette guidelines every Facebook member should follow:

- Include a current, realistic, clean photo of yourself and only yourself in your Profile.

- Proofread your Profile and status updates before posting information.

- Respond to status updates regularly. You don't have to comment on every status update, but do express genuine interest in what's going on in your friends' lives.

- Don't friend just anybody. It cheapens your true friendships and could potentially expose your friends and what they say to people they'd rather not know. In addition, you may be judged by the company you keep and what that company shares on your Wall and in your News Feed.

- Don't over-poke. It gets annoying real fast. (Poking consists of pulling up a friend's Profile by clicking on her name or photo and then clicking the **Poke** link (upper right of the page last we checked). The recipient of the poke receives a message letting her know you've acknowledged her existence. It's kind of dopey, which is why you should do it rarely, if at all.

- Ask for permission before tagging someone in a photo. More about tagging photos in Chapter 7.

- Watch your language. If you wouldn't say it front of your mom or your boss, don't say it on Facebook.

- Go easy on the selling. If you have something to sell, use the Facebook Marketplace (see Chapter 16). Remember, it's called social networking, not social selling.

Help! Navigating Facebook's Help System

Although we cover the most important stuff you need to know to use Facebook, we can't cover everything in such a limited space and, as explained in the introduction, Facebook tends to change. If you need help with something that's not covered in this book or that has changed since we wrote about it, head to Facebook's Help system. Click **Account > Help Center** or click the **Help** link at the bottom of the page. The Facebook Help Center enables you to search for a keyword or question, browse help topics and discussions, view the top questions and their answers, learn more about games, and brush up on Facebook security and safety.

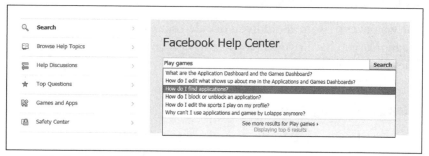

The Facebook Help Center enables you to access different forms of help.

To search for a specific answer, click **Search**, click in the **Enter a keyword or question** box, type a search phrase that best expresses the question you have or the feature you need assistance with, and click **Search**. (As you type, a list of help topics that match what you type appears, and you can click on the topic that's most relevant.) If you typed a word or phrase and clicked **Search**, Facebook displays a collection of links that most closely match your search. Click the link you think is most likely to provide the information you need.

To browse for help, click **Browse Help Topics**, click the feature you need help with, and then follow the trail of links to the solution.

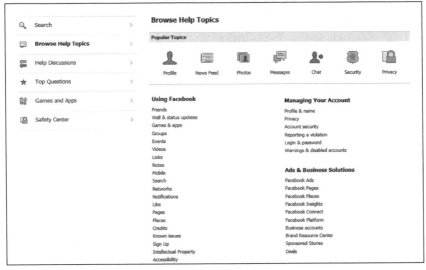

Browse Facebook's Help Topics.

Quitting Facebook

For whatever reason, should you decide that you want out of Facebook, you have two exits: you can deactivate your account or delete it.

Deactivating Your Account

Deactivating your account leaves all your stuff intact. If you quit and get homesick for Facebook, you can always pick up where you left off. To deactivate your account, here's what you do:

1. Click **Account > Account Settings**.

2. In the lower-right corner of the Settings box, click **deactivate**. Facebook displays the guilt screen, complete with photos of all the friends who will miss you very, very much. Don't look.

3. Scroll down the page to the deactivation options.

4. Click the reason that best describes why you're leaving Facebook.

5. (Optional) Click in the **Please explain further** box and type any additional explanation you'd like to pass along to the folks at Facebook. (Be nice, or at least respectful.)

6. (Optional) If you want to stop receiving e-mail notifications from Facebook whenever your friends invite you to do something or send you a message, click **Opt out of receiving future emails from Facebook**.

7. Click the **Confirm** button. Facebook deactivates your account and displays a message informing you how to return later if you change your mind.

The guilt screen.

Deleting Your Account

Deleting an account is a more serious and long-term decision. Everything in your account is erased, including your photos, notes, list of friends, and so on. It's like getting rid of all your stuff and entering a witness-protection program.

If you're sure you want to delete your account, it's pretty simple. Head to https://ssl.facebook.com/help/contact.php?show_form= delete_account, click the **Submit** button, and respond to any confirmation warnings as desired. You're outta there.

The Least You Need to Know

- To get on Facebook, go to www.facebook.com and then complete the Sign Up form and submit it.
- Your News Feed shows status updates, photos, videos, and other stuff that you and your friends have chosen to share.
- To post something to your News Feed and Wall, click in the Publisher (top of the News Feed), type something, and click **Share**.
- To view your Profile, click **Profile** (right end of the top menu).
- To return to the opening page, click the **Facebook** logo on the left end of the top menu or **Home** on the right end.
- You can get help at any time by clicking **Account** (upper-right corner of the screen) and then **Help Center**.

Protecting Your Privacy and Profile

Chapter

2

In This Chapter

- Restricting access to your personal information
- Banning certain members from contacting you
- Protecting yourself from phishers, hackers, spammers, and other lowlifes
- Keeping your e-mail address from falling into the wrong hands

One of the coolest features of Facebook is that it lets you control what others see. You can restrict access to information contained in your Profile, including contact information and where you work or attend school, and prevent certain individuals from posting to your Wall. You also control who can search for you and what they see when they find you, access to certain photo albums, and the information available to applications you use on Facebook.

Before you bare your soul on Facebook, you should be aware of just how private and secure your information is likely to be and any threats that might be lurking on or beyond your Wall. This chapter discusses key privacy and security concerns and shows you how to protect yourself and any sensitive information on Facebook.

Setting Your Privacy Preferences

Although Facebook is open to the public, your life doesn't need to be. Facebook provides privacy settings you can use to restrict or allow access to your information and activities on Facebook. By default, only your Facebook friends have access to most of your Profile information and can see your status updates and various activities you engage in.

In addition, Facebook *never* discloses pokes (except to the person you poke), messages (except to the recipient), whose Profile or photos you view, whose notes you read, groups and events you decline to join, friend requests you ignore or reject, friends you remove, or notes and photos you delete.

WHOA!

Facebook's privacy features are not foolproof. Even if you employ all measures to tighten security, your status updates, photos, videos, and any other information you place on Facebook could fall into the wrong hands and come back to haunt you. People have lost jobs and attracted the attention of law enforcement for what they've posted on Facebook, so follow our advice and share with care.

To access your privacy settings, click **Account** (in the top menu, right side) and click **Privacy Settings**. The Privacy page appears, presenting several groups of related privacy options, along with Block Lists to prevent certain people from contacting you on Facebook. We cover these options in the following sections.

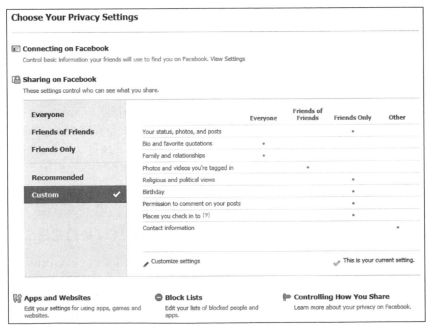

The Privacy Settings page.

Facebook has a long track record of changing the way you access privacy options, so remain flexible. You're likely to encounter the same options described in the following sections, but how you access those options may differ.

Connecting on Facebook

To tighten or relax restrictions on who can view your Profile information, send you friend requests or messages, and view your friend list, access your Privacy Settings page and then, below Connecting on Facebook, click **View Settings**. This displays the Connecting on Facebook privacy page.

You can tighten or relax restrictions on access to specific information.

For most items on this page, you can enter preferences to restrict or open access to Everyone, Friends of Friends, or Friends Only. Items may also include a Customize option with the following additional choices:

- **Specific People:** If you choose this option, a text box appears, prompting you to type the names of friends or one or more of your friend lists you're allowing to access this content.

- **Only Me:** Blocks access to everyone but you.

- **Hide this from:** You can choose Friends of Friends or Only Friends and then exclude individuals on one or more of your friend lists by entering them in this text box.

When you're done entering your preferences in the Custom Privacy dialog box, click **Save Setting**.

To return to the main Privacy page at any time, click **Back to Privacy** (upper left).

Sharing on Facebook

Facebook recommends that you share statuses, photos, posts, your bio and favorite quotations, and your family and relationships with everyone; share photos and videos you're tagged in, religious and political views, and your birthday only with friends and friends of friends; grant permission to comment on your posts and access to places you check in to with friends only; and keep your contact information to yourself. (For more about "checking in" to Facebook Places, see Chapter 15.) To change these settings, click any of the following options on your Privacy Settings page below Sharing on Facebook:

- **Everyone:** Provides everyone on Facebook full access to everything except your contact information.

- **Friends of Friends:** Gives friends of friends access to your status, photos, and posts; your bio and favorite quotations; and photos and videos you're tagged in. Only friends have access to your religious and political views and birthday, permission to comment on your posts, and access to places you check in to. You keep your contact information to yourself.

- **Friends Only:** Gives friends full access to everything about you on Facebook except your contact information.

- **Recommended:** Provides limited access to information according to whether someone is your Facebook friend, a friend of a friend, or a stranger.

- **Custom:** If you changed any settings, click **Custom** to view your current settings.

Click a collection of settings

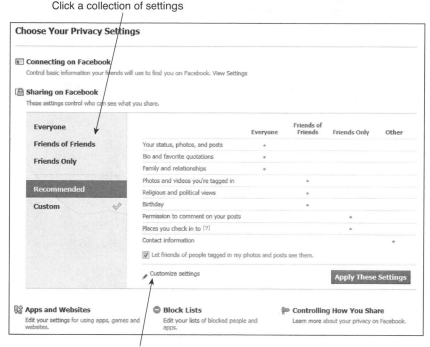

Click **Customize settings** to fine-tune your preferences

Customize your settings.

After choosing a collection of settings, click the **Customize settings** link. This gives you access to additional settings that may not be displayed on the main Privacy Settings screen, such as settings to control what others are permitted to share about you. For these additional settings, you can typically enable or disable the setting; choose to share with everyone, friends of friends, friends only, Only Me, or customize; or click **Edit Settings** for additional options.

The Customize Settings page also enables you to preview your Profile to see it as others will see it. Click the **Preview My Profile** button (upper right). To see what your Profile looks like to a specific friend, click in the **Start typing a friend's name** box, start typing the friend's name, and when you see the person's name, click it.

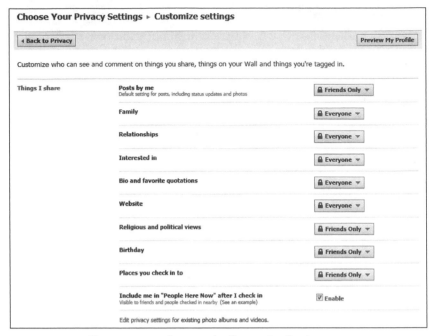

For more control, access the Customize Settings page.

WHOA!

We discourage you from providing access to your e-mail address, even to your Facebook friends. If a hacker obtains your e-mail address, he has half the information he needs to log in to your account and all the information he needs to start spamming you. If you keep your e-mail address hidden, people can contact you by sending you a Facebook message. Then if you want them to have your direct e-mail address, you can e-mail it to them.

To return to the Privacy Settings page, click **Back to Privacy Settings**.

Apps and Websites Privacy

Certain applications and websites require access to your Profile information to do whatever it is they do. Here's a summary of the types of information Facebook gives applications and websites access to and the activities that trigger these permissions:

- If you or one of your friends visits an application or a Facebook-enhanced website, the application or website can access only the information in your public Profile—your name, networks, Profile picture, and friend list—plus any information you choose to make available to "everyone." (A Facebook-enhanced website is one that Facebook does not own or operate but that interfaces with the Facebook platform on a permission basis.)

- When you authorize an application (see Chapter 13), you give it permission to access any information in your account that it requires to work, except for your contact information.

- Facebook requires applications and websites to honor all of your privacy settings.

- If a friend authorizes an application, it can access any information in her account that it requires to work, including your friend's friend list. This means even if you don't authorize the application it has permission to access some of your information, too, specifically your name, Profile picture, gender, networks, user ID, and any other information you've chosen to make accessible to everyone, unless you turn off platform applications and websites, as explained later in this section.

- If you visit a Facebook-enhanced website, it may access information in accordance with the previous rules in this list. If you choose not to proceed with a Facebook-related action on an external website, Facebook deletes any information about you that the site may have collected and sent back to Facebook.

You can restrict application access to some of your information by adjusting the application and website privacy settings. Head to the Privacy page and below Apps and Websites, click **Edit your settings.** Use the available buttons to enter your preferences.

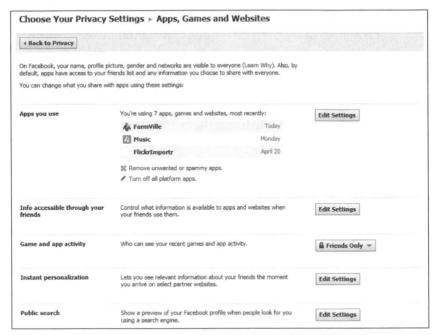

You can restrict application access to your information.

On the Apps, Games and Websites privacy page, you can change the privacy settings for the following options:

- **Apps you use:** You can click **Remove** to remove apps you no longer use, click **Turn off** to turn off one or more platform apps, or click **Edit Settings** to adjust privacy settings for specific applications. (A platform app is an application that runs on Facebook.) If you don't want to use Facebook apps or websites, share information with them, or share information with them through your friends' accounts, click **Turn off all platform apps**, click **Select all**, and click **Turn Off Platform**.

- **Info accessible through your friends:** Your Facebook friends may share information about you with an application or Facebook-enhanced external website. For example, your friend may use a greeting card application that gathers the names and birthdays of all her friends to prompt her to send a card on her friend's birthday. To prevent your friends from sharing certain pieces of information about you, click **Edit Settings** and remove the checkbox next to every piece of information you *don't* want your friends passing along.

- **Game and app activity:** When you and a friend play the same game or use the same application, your activities in these games or applications may show up on one another's accounts and perhaps each other's friends' accounts. To control access to this information, click the button across from this option and click **Everyone > Friends of Friends > Friends Only**, or click **Customize**, use the Custom Privacy dialog box to enter your preferences, and then click **Save Setting**.

- **Instant personalization:** Instant personalization is designed to improve your experience in Facebook's partner sites—for example, by enabling you to interact with Facebook friends who may be visiting the site at the same time and viewing your friends' movie ratings or travel advice on sites that offer those features. If you don't want Facebook sharing your information with these sites, use this option to disable instant personalization.

- **Public search:** If someone searches for you on Google, Yahoo!, or another search site, the site may display a preview of your Facebook Profile. You can use this option to disable public search, so if people want to find you on Facebook, they need to search on Facebook.

Blocking Annoying Individuals

When someone becomes more of a nuisance than a true friend, you may want to block the person entirely. A block prevents the person from viewing your Profile and severs all ties, including friendship connections and friend details. In addition, your Profile won't appear in his searches, and his Profile won't appear in yours. That'll teach him!

WHOA!

Removing someone from your blocked list doesn't automatically restore your friendship. If you want to take the person back as a friend, you'll need to send him a new friend request and grovel for his approval, as discussed in Chapter 4.

The easiest way to block someone is to go to the Privacy Settings page, under Block Lists click **Edit your lists**, click in the **Person** box, type his name, and click **Block This User**. Facebook blocks the person but doesn't notify the person of the block, because that would be downright rude. (You can block a person by e-mail address, instead, which comes in handy if the person isn't a Facebook member yet. Just use the Email box instead of the Person box.)

If the person you want to block is not on your friend list, you have another way to block her. Pull up her Profile and click the **Report/ Block this Person** link (near the bottom of the left column, last time we looked). The **Report and/or block ...** dialog box appears, and you can choose to block the person, report the individual (be sure to select a reason), or both. (To block or report a friend, first de-friend the individual, as explained in Chapter 4.)

You can block or report someone who's not a friend.

Defending Yourself from Hackers and Phishers

Facebook does a fairly good job of policing activity and cracking down on inappropriate behavior, but hackers, stalkers, schemers, and scammers have been known to ply their trade on the platform. To protect yourself, your information, and your account from these miscreants, you should be aware of the potential threats and practice some safe Facebooking strategies.

Keeping Hackers from Hijacking Your Account

A malicious hacker may be able to hijack your Facebook account and then pose as you. Once they gain access, they can do anything from posting tasteless jokes in your News Feed to e-mailing your friends requesting a money transfer or credit card information so you can fly back home from Bora Bora, where you've been robbed and held captive for 36 hours.

To protect your account and information from hackers, consider practicing the following safeguards:

- Change your password to something that's difficult for hackers to guess. Include both letters and numbers, and make it fairly long—10 to 14 characters is better than 6 to 8. Use a different password than you use for other online accounts. Remember, passwords are case sensitive. To access the form for changing your password, click **Account** (in the top menu), **Account Settings**, and then, across from Password, click **Change**.

- Change your password every three months or so.

- If other people have access to the computer you use to log in to Facebook, log out whenever you're done using Facebook. Also, don't use your browser's "remember" feature to store your username and password.

- Include as little sensitive information as possible in your Profile; if a hacker does gain access, he won't have your name, address, phone number, and other potentially sensitive information.

- Don't give your login information to anyone for any reason. Hackers may pose as Facebook representatives to trick you into passing along your login information. See the next section, "Dodging Phishing Schemes," for details.

- Download only programs you fully trust. Hackers can embed code in an otherwise harmless application that captures the keystrokes you press to log in and then sends those keystrokes to the hacker.

- Add a security question to your account, so if it does get hijacked, you'll have an easier time regaining access to it. To access the form for adding or changing a security question, click **Account** (in the top menu), click **Account Settings**, and then click **Security Question**. (After you enter your security question, this option disappears and is no longer available, so if you don't see it, that's probably what happened.)

FRIEND-LY ADVICE

If your account has been hacked, try logging in to Facebook and changing your password. If the hacker already changed your password so you can't log in, go to www.facebook.com, click the **Forgot your password?** link, and follow the on-screen instructions to reset your password. You must have access to one of the e-mail accounts associated with your Facebook account, so Facebook can send you a new password. If you don't have access to one of those e-mail accounts, you can use your security question/answer to regain access to your Facebook account.

Dodging Phishing Schemes

Phishing scams dangle a line in front of you, hoping you'll take the bait. In this case, the bait is usually an e-mail alert warning you of some problem with your account. The alert typically contains a link you can click to go to a site where you can learn more and address the issue. The site typically looks official and matches what you expect to see—in this case, a Facebook-like interface. You think you're on Facebook, but you're really on a website the phisher created and, before you can fix the problem, you have to log in.

Unfortunately, if you do try to log in, you pass your Facebook login information directly to the phisher, who can then log in to your real Facebook account, change your password, access your Profile information, pose as you, and cause all sorts of trouble.

To defend yourself against phishing schemes, practice the following maneuvers:

- Trust your instincts. If something looks or sounds a little phishy, it probably is.

- Keep in mind that just because something appears to be coming from a friend, it may not be. Your friend's account may have been hijacked.

- Compare the URL in the link with the one that appears in your browser or e-mail program's status bar when you rest the mouse pointer on the link. The link may show www.facebook. com but take you to an entirely different site. You can tell where a link is really going to take you by hovering the mouse pointer over the link and looking in the status bar.

- Keep in mind that Facebook will never send you an e-mail message asking for your login information. If someone's asking for it, they're bad guys.

- If it looks as though someone has hijacked a friend's account and is posing as him, contact your friend immediately.

- Report any suspected phishing scams to Facebook so management can investigate and shut down the perpetrators. At the top of every message you receive is a Report link you can click to report the suspicious message to Facebook. More details about reporting Facebook violations are provided later in this chapter.

Preventing and Stopping Spam

We haven't seen a great deal of spam on Facebook, probably because the service and its members do such a fine job of policing members and advertisers. If you do receive a message on Facebook that appears to be spam, click the **Report Spam** link above the message and follow the on-screen instructions to report the spammer.

Keep in mind that if you're receiving spam that has supposedly originated from a Facebook friend, your friend's account probably has been hijacked.

Reporting Scams and Schemes to Facebook

Facebook monitors members and the activities they engage in, but it relies on members like you to call attention to any abuse of the service. If you notice any lewd, crude, or potentially criminal activity on Facebook, report it. Following are various ways to file a report:

- **Click a Report link and follow the on-screen instructions.** Facebook displays the Report link in various places, including below the Profiles of members who are not your friends, above any open messages, above photos, in notes, and in groups.

- **E-mail abuse@facebook.com.** You can send an e-mail message to Facebook to report suspected member violations.

- **E-mail advertise@facebook.com.** Send an e-mail message to report any suspected abuse by advertisers on Facebook.

When notifying Facebook of suspected violations, be as specific as possible. Identify the member or advertiser by name and describe the violation and where you observed it. Provide a link or URL (page address), if possible.

A Word to Parents ...

Kids love Facebook almost as much as they love their cell phones—maybe more. Unfortunately, some kids are too naïve, and others too worldly, for their own good. Therefore, parents need to lay down the rules and enforce them to keep children out of harm's way.

Review Facebook's safety advice with your child. Click **Account > Help Center** (in the top menu) and then click the **Safety** tab (left menu). You may want to work through this chapter with your child to make sure you've reviewed the privacy preferences and adjusted them to your comfort level.

Following are some words of wisdom to share with your teenager (kids under 13 are prohibited from joining Facebook—unless they lie about their age):

- Don't post your phone number, home address, school name, or any other information a stranger could use to track you down. Facebook's privacy features may not fully protect this information, so don't add it to your Profile.

- Don't friend strangers. Friend only people you already know and trust from your real-world encounters.

- Don't agree to face-to-face meetings with people you don't already know and trust in the real world.

- Don't believe everything a person says about himself in his Profile or otherwise. On the Internet, a 50-year-old child abuser can pass himself off as a 17-year-old Romeo.

- Report any inappropriate content or communications to your parents and to Facebook at abuse@facebook.com.

WHOA!

You can install computer nanny software to provide some level of protection, but no system is failsafe. Place the family computer(s) in a common area, where you can supervise your kids' computer use without seeming like you're hovering. Limit computer use to normal hours when you're awake and alert. Sticking a computer in a kid's room where they can loiter on Facebook 24/7 is neither healthy nor safe.

The Least You Need to Know

- Check and adjust your privacy settings. Know what you're sharing, and restrict access to anything you don't want to share.

- To access the privacy settings, click **Account** and then click **Privacy Settings**.

- Consider removing your home address and phone number from your Profile and not sharing your e-mail address with anyone, especially if you're under the age of 18.

- Keep hackers at bay by using a password that's tough to guess and then changing it every three months or so.

- Never click a link in a message or post and then enter your username and password or other sensitive information; it could be a phishing scam.
- Report any violations or suspicious activity to Facebook.

Fleshing Out Your Personal Profile

In This Chapter

- Creating and editing your personal Profile
- Swapping out your Profile photograph
- Writing something clever about yourself
- Tweaking your personal and contact information

Without a personal Profile on Facebook, all you are is a name without a face, a skeleton, a nobody. Add a few details, including a photo, a brief bio, and some juicy personal and professional tidbits, and all of a sudden, you're somebody! In this chapter, we show you how to put some meat on those bones and hang a face on that name by filling out your Facebook Profile.

Accessing Your Profile to Adjust It

Before you can start tweaking your Profile, you have to get to it. In Facebook, the following three paths take you to the page where you can edit your Profile:

- Click **Profile** in the top menu at the top of any page and then click the **Edit Profile** button.
- Click your name or **Edit My Profile** at the top of the column to the left of your News Feed.

- Click your photo or photo placeholder anywhere you see it in Facebook and then click the **Edit Profile** button.

However you choose to get there, your Profile page appears. In the left column, click the item you want to edit, and then enter your changes on the right.

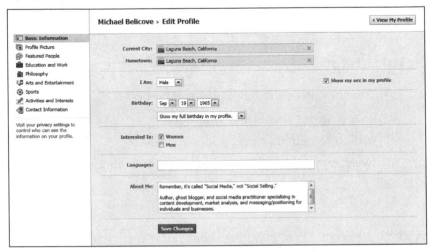

Your Profile page looks something like this.

WHOA!

Be careful what you include as part of your Profile. By default, friends and anyone in the networks you join (see Chapter 4) can view the information in your Profile, including your birthday, hometown, and relationship status. Your friends can view most of your contact information, too, including your phone number and address. To find out how to restrict access to this information, flip back to Chapter 2.

Changing Your Profile Photo

You can add or change your Profile photo at any time by uploading a new photo or snapping a photo with a webcam attached to your computer. As soon as you change photos, Facebook updates your photo in your Profile and wherever else it appears on Facebook, including your status updates—past, present, and future.

Prior to your photo shoot, review the following guidelines and suggestions for Profile photos:

- No porn—hard, soft, or otherwise.

- Use a current photo; making the wrinkles disappear by uploading an old high school photo is cheating.

- Use a photo of yourself; trying to pass yourself off as someone else is a violation of Facebook's terms of use.

- If someone else is in the photo, crop out that person. Otherwise, your friends may have to guess which one is you.

- Use a quality photo. If it's too dark, for example, use a photo-editing program to lighten it. Don't use a blurry photo; no amount of editing can fix a bad shot.

Uploading a Digital Photo

One of the best ways to add a Profile photo is to take a photo using a digital camera or scan in a photo of yourself. You can then adjust the brightness and contrast, if necessary; crop out any distractions in the background; save the image to your computer; and then upload it by following these steps:

1. Click **Profile** in the top menu. Facebook displays your Profile page.

2. Mouse over your photo or photo placeholder. The Change Picture link appears.

3. Click **Change Picture**. The Edit Profile page appears with the Profile Picture tab selected.

4. Click the **Browse** button. A file upload dialog box appears.

5. Navigate to the disk drive and folder that contains the file you want to use.

6. Click the file's name.

7. Click **Open**. Facebook uploads the file (which can take a few seconds to a few minutes depending on the speed of your Internet connection and the size of the file).

8. Click **Edit Thumbnail**. The Edit Thumbnail box appears.

9. Drag the image to center yourself inside the box.

10. Click **Save**.

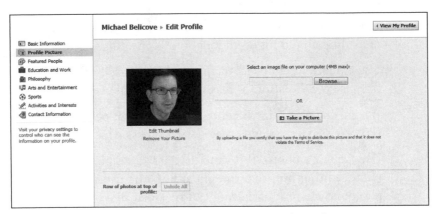

You can upload a photo or snap one with a webcam.

Snapping a Photo with Your Webcam

If you have a functioning webcam, you can take a photo of yourself sitting at your computer and have Facebook upload it to your Profile.

> **FRIEND-LY ADVICE**
>
> When snapping your own mug shot, look directly into the webcam instead of at your computer screen or you'll look like you're staring at the ground or up in the sky.

To snap a photo with your webcam, here's what you do:

1. Click **Profile** in the top menu. Facebook displays your Profile page.

2. Mouse over your photo. The Change Picture link appears.

3. Click **Change Picture**. The Edit Profile page appears with the Profile Picture tab selected.

4. Click **Take a Picture**. The Take a Profile Picture dialog box appears.

5. If a box appears asking whether Facebook can access your camera and microphone, click **Allow** and then **Close**.

6. Click the **Camera** icon and strike a pose. Facebook counts down three seconds and snaps your photo.

7. Preview your photo, and then do one of the following:

    If you don't like what you see, click the **X** in the upper-right corner of the picture and go back to Step 6 to reshoot.

    If the photo is acceptable, click **Save Picture**. Facebook uploads the file, which can take a few seconds to a few minutes.

8. Click **Edit Thumbnail**. The Edit Thumbnail box appears.

9. Drag the image to center yourself inside the box.

10. Click **Save**.

The Take a Profile Picture dialog box prompts you to snap a photo of yourself by clicking the camera icon.

Selecting a Picture for Your Profile

As you upload Profile photos from your computer and shoot Profile photos using a webcam, Facebook places them in your Profile Pictures album. You can then select which Profile photo you want to use.

To choose a different photo from your collection, click **Profile** in the top menu, click **Photos** (below your Profile photo), and click the **Profile Pictures** album. Click the photo you want to use, and click **Make Profile Picture**. Facebook may ask you to crop the photo for use as a thumbnail and/or confirm your choice of photo, after which the photo you just selected appears in your Profile and status updates.

You can delete a Profile photo by performing these same steps, clicking the option to delete the photo, and giving your confirmation. For more details on managing your photos, check out Chapter 7.

You can make the selected photo your Profile picture.

Clipping Your Thumbnail

When you post a Profile photo, Facebook fits it inside the little box allocated for your mug shot. You don't have any control over how much of your photo is visible, but you do have some control over how it fits in the box.

Click **Profile**, mouse over your photo, click **Change Picture**, and click **Edit Thumbnail**. In the Edit Thumbnail dialog box, move the mouse pointer over the picture until the four-headed arrow appears, then drag the thumbnail up, down, left, or right to change its position in the box. When it looks just right, release the mouse button and click **Save**.

Drag your photo in the preview box.

Hiding and Unhiding the Photos in the Photostream

At the top of your Profile is a Photostream that displays photos in which you've been recently tagged (see Chapter 7) or your Profile photos. To remove a photo without deleting it, mouse over the photo and click the **X** that appears in its upper-right corner. If you remove all of the photos, the Photostream collapses, providing more room for displaying Wall posts.

If you change your mind, you can restore all of the photos you hid. Click **Profile > Edit Profile > Profile Picture**, and then click the **Unhide All** button.

You can remove photos from the Photostream.

Editing Information About Yourself

When you registered with Facebook, you entered a little information about yourself to get started. You can edit and add to this information at any time to flesh out your Profile. To edit your Profile, click **Profile** and then click **Edit My Profile**.

Your Edit Profile page appears with several options off to the left, including Basic Information, Featured People, Education and Work, Philosophy, and Activities and Interests. Click one of the options to edit its information, as described in the following sections.

Basic Information

Basic Information goes slightly beyond name, rank, and serial number. It includes your Sex (and whether to display it in your Profile), Current City, Hometown, Birthday, Languages you speak, and a couple other items of interest. Simply complete the form as you would fill out any online form and click **Save Changes**.

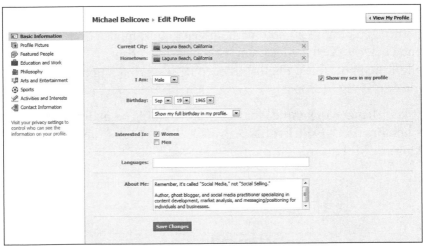

You can edit, add, or remove basic information about yourself.

Featured People

If you have a friend or family member you want to feature in your Profile, such as a parent, child, or sibling, first "friend" the person, as explained in Chapter 4. Then display your Edit Profile page and click **Featured People** (left column). The Featured People page appears, enabling you to specify the following:

- **Relationship Status:** Regardless of whether you're involved with a significant other, open this list and choose your current relationship status. If you're in a relationship, you have the option to specify with whom; click in the box below the drop-down list, and start typing the person's name. As you type, a list appears showing the names of your Facebook friends who match what you've typed. When you see the name of your significant other, click it. If you don't see a match, Facebook will prompt you for the person's e-mail address (after you choose to save your changes) so it can send the person an invitation to join Facebook.

- **Family:** To feature a family member, click in the text box next to Family and start typing the person's name. As you type, a list appears showing the names of your Facebook friends who match what you've typed. When you see your relative's name, click it. Then, open the **Select Relation** list and click the description of how the person is related to you.

- **Friends:** To feature a list of friends or colleagues, click **Add an existing list or group**, click the checkbox next to each list or group you want to add, and click **Add**. Or click **Create new list** and create a new list, as explained in Chapter 4.

When you're done entering your preferences, click **Save Changes**.

POKE

You add a family member only by entering the name of the person you want to add. You can't just say you have a son or daughter, for example, without supplying the name of your son or daughter.

Education and Work

When you signed up for Facebook, it asked for information about schools you attended and places you worked. Facebook can use this information to help you track down friends and help classmates and co-workers find you.

If you skipped that part, or would like to edit or add entries, you can do so at any time. Just head to your Profile, click the link to edit it, click **Education and Work**, and enter your changes. The only thing that's likely to be confusing here is the With box. This enables you to enter Facebook friends who worked or went to school with you. Click in the **With** box and start typing the person's name. As you type, a list appears showing the names of your Facebook friends who match what you've typed. When you see the person's name, click it. If the person isn't a Facebook friend, Facebook prompts you for the person's e-mail address so it can send the person an invitation to join Facebook.

In the Education and Work section, you can also add or remove schools or jobs.

Personal Information

When you're ready to get personal with your friends, you'll want to share more details about yourself, including, perhaps, your religious and political affiliations; quotations you like; favorite music, books, movies, television shows, and games; favorite sports, teams, and athletes; and hobbies, activities, and interests. You can share any or all of this information by opening your Edit Profile page, clicking the desired option in the left column, completing the form, and saving your changes.

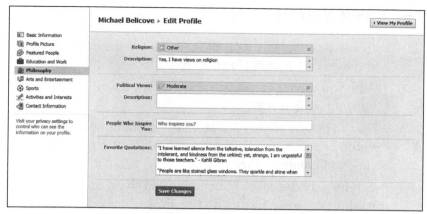

You can get personal by sharing your philosophy, views, and more.

Contact Information

If you want your friends to be able to get in touch with you outside the confines of Facebook, include your contact information. Facebook already has the e-mail address you used to register, but you can add phone numbers, your mailing address, your website address, and even IM (instant messaging) screen names. Just click **Contact Information** on your Edit Profile page and supply as much or as little contact information as you like.

WHOA!

Share with care. We recommend omitting your home address and phone numbers. If a friend wants to call or visit, they can e-mail you to request that information. Sure, given your full name and hometown, just about anyone can track you down, but you don't have to make it easy for just anyone to show up on your doorstep or call you on your phone. For additional details on protecting your privacy, check out Chapter 2.

The Least You Need to Know

- To edit your Profile, click **Profile** (in the top menu of any page) and then click **Edit My Profile**.
- After you choose to edit your Profile, click the tab for the section you want to edit.
- Upload or change your Profile image by mousing over your photo or photo placeholder on your Edit Profile page and clicking **Change Picture**.
- Carefully choose which information you share, but include enough for family, friends, and co-workers to find and friend you.

Connecting with Friends, Family, and Classmates

In This Chapter

- Sharing with Facebook friends
- Scouring Facebook and beyond for people you know
- Making and managing friends
- Exposing yourself to more potential friends

In real life, you're not just you. You are the sum total of yourself, your past, your aspirations, and everyone with whom you interact, including friends, family members, colleagues, and even those strangers you're about to meet.

The same is true on Facebook, only more so. When you first register and log in, all you are is a name. When you start to connect with friends, family members, colleagues, and former classmates—and they start connecting with you—you become part of a thriving community. Each new Facebook friend adds a stitch to the tapestry that's you. In short, to get anything *out of* Facebook, you need to get *into* Facebook and get connected. This chapter shows you how.

Knowing What It Means to Be a Friend

On Facebook, your friends have benefits that others on Facebook may not have, depending on your privacy settings (see Chapter 2). They can read your Profile and follow discussions among you and your other friends, for example. When you "friend" someone on Facebook, you give them access to information about yourself and perhaps your friends that could be sensitive or confidential, so you'd better have a pretty clear idea of who your friends are and what you're sharing with them before you start adding people to your inner circle.

WHOA!

You have complete control over what appears on your Facebook Wall and what's shared among friends, as explained in Chapter 2. Until you review your privacy settings, choose your friends and what you share very carefully and assume everything you post is publicly accessible. If you receive a friend request from someone you don't know, ignore it for now.

Sharing Walls and News Feeds

Friends share News Feeds and Walls, which may seem a little odd right now, but you'll get the idea in Chapter 5. For now, just keep in mind that whatever you post in your News Feed shows up on your friends' News Feeds and vice versa. In other words, if you add your mom as a friend, she'll be able to see whatever you post in your News Feed. Post a message about the wild time you had at that party Friday night, and Mom can see it.

Your Wall is a quieter place, displaying only your posts and anything your friends have specifically posted to your Wall. However, whatever you or your friends post on your Wall or you post on theirs may show up in your News Feed and theirs. In Chapter 5, you learn more about the Wall and News Feed.

Sharing Photo Albums

When you upload photos to your account, your friends have access to those photos. You can restrict access to photos, as Chapter 7 explains, but until you learn how to do that, hold off on posting anything too risqué or revealing. Even if your photos are accessible only to your friends, they might decide to share those photos with others—some of whom you might not want looking at those photos.

Friends can also "tag" you in a photo that they or someone they know has uploaded to Facebook. Tagging means that the photo is labeled with your name and will link to your Profile, which is kind of cool until someone tags you in an embarrassing pose (or embarrassing clothes—oh, those '80s!) and that tag is broadcast to all your friends, family, and co-workers. In Chapter 2, we show you how to keep those tag notifications to yourself. In Chapter 7, you learn how to add and remove tags.

Sharing Information

Unless you indicate otherwise, most of your Profile information is readily accessible to all your Facebook friends. This includes Basic Information, Personal Information, Contact Information (address, phone number, but not your e-mail address, unless you choose to share it), Education and Work experience, and a list of any groups you've joined. (See Chapter 9 for more about the Groups feature.)

In Chapter 2, you learn how to hide sensitive information from prying eyes. Until then, become friends only with people you don't mind having access to your information.

Digging Up People You Know

The whole purpose of Facebook is to facilitate connections among people, and since you have to find people before you can connect with them, Facebook features several ways to locate the people you know ... assuming, of course, they're on Facebook.

What about all those folks you know who aren't on Facebook yet? No worries—Facebook provides a way to invite them to join!

After you make a few friends, Facebook may display friends of theirs and suggest that you invite them to be your friends. All you need to do is click the person's name in the Suggestions box or the "We'd like to help you find your friends" page, and follow the on-screen cues to send a friend request. More information on sending a friend request is provided later in this chapter.

Searching for an Individual by Name or E-Mail

One of the easiest ways to dig up a specific individual on Facebook is to perform a search. Click in the **Search** box (top menu) and start typing the person's name or e-mail address. As you type, the names of Facebook members appear that match what you've typed so far. If you see the person's name, click it to access the person's Profile page. You can then click the **Add as Friend** button to send a friend request.

If you finish typing and the person you're looking for doesn't pop up, press **Enter** or click the **Search** button (the magnifying glass to the right of the Search box). Facebook displays possible matches. If the person still doesn't show up, use another search method described in this chapter.

> **FRIEND-LY ADVICE**
>
> If you know the person's e-mail address, try searching for that instead of the person's name. An e-mail address is more likely to turn up the individual you're looking for and screen out all others with similar names.

Searching for People in Your E-Mail Address Book

Facebook can use your e-mail address book to track down people you already keep in touch with. You can import addresses from a web-based e-mail account, such as Google Mail or Yahoo! Mail, or directly from Microsoft Outlook. If you use some other e-mail program or don't want to give Facebook access to your web-based e-mail account, you can export the address book from your e-mail program, save it as a file to your computer, and then import the addresses into Facebook.

Following are the steps for importing addresses from a web-based e-mail program. (After these steps, we cover a couple variations you'll run into if you're using a different type of e-mail program or would rather not give Facebook access to your web-based account.) Here's what you do:

1. Click **Find Friends** in the top menu. Your Friends page appears.

2. Scroll down to the web-based e-mail service you use and click **Find Friends** next to it. (If your e-mail service isn't listed, click **Find Friends** next to Other Email Service.)

3. Enter the e-mail address you use to log in to your web-based e-mail program and click **Find Friends**. Facebook prompts you to enter your username and password for that service.

4. Enter your username and password for the web-based e-mail service and click the button to sign in. Your service may display a prompt, through Facebook, asking you to confirm.

5. If prompted to confirm, click the option to give your okay. Facebook retrieves and then displays a list of any Facebook members who've registered using any of the e-mail addresses in your address book.

6. Click the contacts you want to add as friends. (You can deselect contacts by clicking them again.)

7. Select any of your contacts not on Facebook that you want to invite. Facebook will invite nonmembers to become members so they can be your Facebook friends.

8. Click **Add as Friends**. Facebook will e-mail your friend request to everyone you selected.

Facebook can log in to your web-based e-mail program and import your e-mail addresses.

FRIEND-LY ADVICE

In addition to finding people you e-mail, Facebook can help you find people on popular services, including Skype.

If you have a PC running Windows and use Outlook, Outlook Express, or Windows Live Mail to manage your e-mail, open the Find Friends page and next to Other Tools click **Find Friends**. Click **Find My Windows Contacts**, and follow the on-screen prompts to complete the operation. Facebook scours your PC for a contacts file and displays a list of Facebook members who've registered with any of the addresses. Select the contacts you want to add as friends, click **Add as Friends**, and follow the on-screen instructions to complete the operation.

If that didn't work or you use some other e-mail client on your computer, such as Mozilla Thunderbird, next to Other Email Service, click **Find Friends**, and then click the **How to create a contact file … link**. This displays a list of links you can click for instructions on how to export an address book from any of several popular e-mail programs. Click the link for your e-mail program and follow the instructions to export your contact file.

After exporting your contact file, head back to your Find Friends page. Click **Browse**, use the resulting dialog box to select the e-mail address file you want to import, click **Open**, and then click **Find Friends**. Select the name of each person you want to invite to be your friend, and click **Add as Friends**.

Finding Friends, Classmates, and Co-Workers

When fleshing out your Profile, as explained in Chapter 3, you may have specified schools from which you graduated, your hometown, the town where you're currently living, and places where you've worked or are currently working. Assuming other Facebook members entered matching information into their Profiles, you can have Facebook track them down for you.

Click **Find Friends** in the top menu. Scroll to the bottom of the section for adding personal contacts as friends, click **Other Tools**, and click **Find Friends > Classmates and Coworkers**. Facebook displays a bunch of Facebook members you may know based on information you entered about yourself (and they entered about themselves) or whether you have a mutual Facebook friend.

Click checkboxes next to options on the left to filter (narrow) the list to mutual friends of one or more current Facebook friends, people from your hometown and/or current city, those who've attended the same school as you have, and/or people who've worked for the same employer. You may check more than one box to narrow the list even more; for example, you may want to search for people who've attended the same high school and college or find out whether anyone you're working with now is from the same hometown.

When you find someone you want to friend, send the person a friend request, as explained next.

Find friends, classmates, and co-workers.

WHOA!

Think twice about friending colleagues and co-workers. We've heard plenty of stories about co-workers passing along embarrassing and sometimes career-ending status updates that other co-workers and even the boss ended up reading. If you do friend a colleague, be especially careful about anything you post about your job, office politics, or other colleagues.

Seeing Who Your Friends Are

If you can't recall who you've friended or need to access a friend's Profile page and you don't see that friend's name or picture, you can pull up a list of your friends by clicking **Friends** (in the left menu).

The Friends option works very differently depending on whether you click it on your Home or Profile page. Click **Home** and then **Friends**, and the page that appears displays any friend requests you haven't yet responded to, a section for adding personal contacts as friends, a People You May Know section, and an Edit Friends button. To view your friends, click **Edit Friends** and then click the **See All Friends** link.

A quicker way to access your friends is to click **Profile** and then click **Friends** (in the left menu). You now see a list of your friends, including their names and photos.

> **FRIEND-LY ADVICE**
>
> If you have lots of friends, you can narrow the list. Click **Home** or **Profile** (top menu), click **Friends** (left menu), and click **Edit Friends** (upper right). Click the **Recently Interacted** button above the list of friends and choose the desired option: All Friends, Recently Interacted, Recently Added, Search by Current City, Search by Hometown, Search by School, Search by Workplace, or Search by Interest. If you chose one of the Search by options, click in the text box next to the button and type the name of the city, hometown, school, workplace, or interest, and press **Enter**.

Befriending and De-Friending

Becoming friends on Facebook requires mutual consent. One member initiates the process by sending a friend request. The other member must then accept the invitation to confirm the arrangement.

In the following sections, you discover how to send and respond to friend requests, de-friend someone with whom you no longer wish to associate, and group your friends using friend lists to help you navigate your various social circles.

Sending a Friend Request

You can bump into prospective friends all sorts of ways on Facebook. Someone can send you a friend request, you can track down the person by performing a search, your current friends can offer suggestions, or Facebook may display a list of suggested friends.

However you happen to bump into a person, the process for inviting them to become your friend is always the same: click **Add as Friend** and use the resulting dialog box to send your request. You can click **Send Request** or click **Add a personal message** and type a greeting before clicking **Send Request**. We recommend adding a personal message to each friend request to make the person feel you really care and aren't just padding your friend list.

Your friend must confirm your request before Facebook establishes a connection.

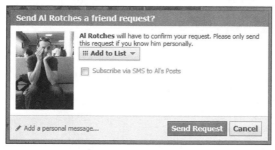

Send a friend request to initiate a new friendship.

Responding to a Friend Request

When someone sends you a friend request, you typically receive an e-mail message with a link you can click to go to Facebook and respond to the request. If you don't check your e-mail very often or have chosen not to receive e-mail notifications, you can check for incoming friend requests by logging on to Facebook and clicking the **Friend Requests** link in the top menu, and then clicking **See All Friend Requests**.

Every friend request includes the person's name and the number of friends you have in common, if any. You can click the person's name or photo to check out her Profile or click the **Mutual Friends** link (if available) to find out which friends you have in common.

After accessing the Friend Requests list, you can click one of the following options to confirm or not:

- **Confirm**, to accept the invitation and become friends.

- **Not Now**, to disregard the invitation. This hides the invitation, and you can return to it later on your Friend Requests page. It also provides an option for deleting the request if you don't know the person. Don't worry, Facebook is polite. It doesn't send the person a rejection slip or anything like that.

If you're not sure whether you know the person, you can always send the person a message to find out how the person knows you and why he sent a friend request. Just click the person's name or photo to access his Profile page, click **Send Message**, and use the resulting dialog box to send your message. See Chapter 6 for more about Facebook's Messages feature.

You can confirm or ignore a friend request.

Dumping a Friend

If you've added a friend by mistake, or decide later that you really don't want the person hanging out in your Face-space, you can de-friend the person. Here's what you do:

1. Click **Account** (in the top menu) and click **Edit Friends**.

2. Click **See All Friends**.

3. Click the **X** next to the person's name. The remove friend dialog box appears, prompting you to confirm.

4. Click **Remove from Friends** to de-friend the person or **Cancel** to give them another chance.

> **FRIEND-LY ADVICE**
>
> Even though Facebook doesn't notify your friend of your decision to de-friend, it can result in an awkward situation if your former friend tries to post something to your Wall and can't get to it. If you decide to re-friend, you have to go through the whole friend-request thing again, which could raise some questions.

Creating and Managing Friend Lists

If you're like most people, you have multiple social circles—family members, grade school classmates, high school classmates, co-workers and colleagues, and perhaps even members of your reading club. Unfortunately, your News Feed shows a mish-mash of all your friends' posts and updates, making the task of sorting out communications within each social circle nearly impossible.

Facebook's Friend List feature can make your social circles more manageable by assigning your friends to individual lists. After creating a friend list, you can use it to do the following:

- When viewing your News Feed (see Chapter 5), click a friend list to hide posts from everyone except the friends on the selected list.

- Send an e-mail message to everyone on the friend list without having to address it to each and every individual. (See Chapter 6 for more about Facebook's Messages feature.)

- Send an event announcement and invitation to everyone on the friend list without having to address it to each and every individual. (See Chapter 11.)

- Tighten or loosen restrictions on your Profile for different friend lists. (See Chapter 2 for more about Facebook privacy settings.)

Consider starting with some basic lists, such as having a separate list for each of the following circles: family members, friends, and co-workers.

WHOA!

A friend list merely filters what appears in your News Feed. Don't make the common mistake of believing that you can post status updates to one friend list without your other friends seeing it. All of your friends are privy to whatever you post, unless you edit the Custom Privacy setting for the status update in question. See Chapter 5 for details about changing privacy settings for individual posts.

To create a friend list and assign some friends to it, here's what you do:

1. Click **Account** (in the top menu), then click **Edit Friends** from the drop-down menu.

2. Above the list of friends, click **+ Create a List**. The Create New List dialog box appears.

3. Click in the **Enter a name** box and type a name for the list, such as Co-Workers, Family, or People I Used to Date.

4. Scroll through the names and images and click each friend you want to include in this list. (If you click a friend by mistake, click the friend again to deselect her.) If your friend list is really long and difficult to scroll through, you can type each friend's name and select each friend that way instead.

5. Click **Create List**. Facebook creates the list and displays it in the left menu, under Lists.

You can edit a friend list at any time. Click **Account > Edit Friends**. In the left menu, click the friend list you want to edit, and then click the **Edit List** button (above the list). This displays a dialog box in which you can change the name of the list and add or remove people.

You can create a friend list and assign friends to it.

To delete an entire friend list, click **Account > Edit Friends**. In the left menu, click the friend list you want to delete and then click **Delete List** (below the list of friends last time we checked). Facebook displays a dialog box warning that deleting the list isn't reversible and asking for your confirmation. Click **Delete List** to confirm or **Cancel** to abort the operation.

POKE

Although deleting a list is irreversible, it doesn't permanently remove your friends from your complete list of friends, so you can always re-create the list—assuming you remember who was on it.

Expanding Your Reach with Networks

A Facebook network is a closed community for a workplace or school that enables members of that community to network in a more private environment. The network enables everyone in it to track down one another more easily and relax restrictions on what they want to share only with members of that network. Facebook allows you to join up to five different networks.

> **WHOA!**
>
> All members of a network must have an authenticated e-mail address for that community; for example, if you want to join the Purdue University network, you need a Purdue University–approved e-mail address that ends in something like @purdue.edu. Facebook must validate the e-mail address before granting you access to the network.

To join a network, here's what you do:

1. Click **Account** (in the top menu) and click **Account Settings**. The Account Settings page appears.

2. Click the **Networks** tab.

3. Click in the **Join a network** box and start typing the name of your workplace, city, state, high school, or college. As you type, Facebook displays networks that match what you've typed so far.

4. Click the name of the network you want to join.

5. Click in the Network e-mail address text box and type the e-mail address you have on that network.

6. Click **Join Network**. Facebook updates the Networks page to show that you're now an active member of the network you just joined.

Joining a network makes your Profile accessible to network members, regardless of whether they're Facebook friends, so you may want to adjust your privacy settings for networks, as explained in Chapter 2.

You can join one or more networks to use Facebook in a sequestered community.

If you join only one network, it becomes your primary network. Whenever you perform a search, results from that network appear first in the search results. If you join two or more networks, only one can be your primary network. To change your primary network, open your **Account Settings** page, click the **Networks** tab, and click the **Make Primary** link next to the desired network.

You can leave a network at any time. Click **Settings > Account Settings**, and the **Networks** tab, and then click **Leave Network** next to the network you want to leave.

Introducing Your Friends

If you think two of your friends may enjoy knowing one another, consider introducing them. To introduce friends, head to the Profile page of the person to whom you want to introduce one or more of your friends and click the **Suggest Friends** button (upper right). (If the button doesn't appear, your friend is not accepting friend requests.) The Suggest Friends for <Name> dialog box appears, prompting you to select some friends. Click each friend you want to introduce to this person, and then click the **Send Suggestions** button.

Introduce your friends to one another.

The Least You Need to Know

- Be selective when friending people on Facebook. Friends can view and access each other's status updates, Walls, and other content.

- To search for someone on Facebook, click in the **Search** box (top menu), type the person's e-mail address or name, and press **Enter**.

- To find more friends on Facebook, click **Account** (top menu), **Find Friends**, and use the resulting options to track down people you may know.

- When you receive a friend request, you have two options: Confirm and Not Now.

- Use friend lists to group friends and reduce some of the clutter in your News Feed.

- To dump a friend, click **Friends** (left menu) > **Edit Friends**, and then **See All**, and click **X** next to the name of the person you want to de-friend.

Hitting the Wall ...
and Your News Feed

In This Chapter

- Understanding the difference between your Wall and News Feed
- Configuring your Wall and filtering its content
- Creating and posting status updates
- Commenting on friends' status updates
- Posting messages on friends' Walls
- Sharing your friends' content with other friends

Facebook provides two major modes of communication between and among friends—the Wall and News Feed. Your News Feed greets you whenever you log on. It's the column in the middle of the screen that asks, "What's on your mind?" and displays recent status updates your friends have posted, along with other information—such as when a friend edits his Profile or takes a quiz. If you wander away from your News Feed, you can always return to it by clicking **Home** or **Facebook** in the top menu.

Your Wall, on the other hand, is a more intimate place that displays only your posts, anything your friends have specifically posted to your Wall, and any Wall-to-Wall discussions you're having with a specific friend. You can view your Wall at any time by clicking **Profile** (in the top menu) or clicking your name or photo in the left menu.

When you click a friend's name, you're taken to that friend's Profile page, where you can read his Wall posts and post messages to this particular friend. As you reply to one another's Wall posts, you engage in a Wall-to-Wall discussion that appears on both your Walls.

In the following sections, you get a better feel for your News Feed and Wall, as you navigate, post status updates, and customize these two areas.

Homing In on Your News Feed

You can't miss your News Feed. Log on to Facebook, and it's right there, in your face, front and center. To filter out some of the "noise" and focus on the most important news of the day, Facebook's default setting for the News Feed is Top News. Facebook hides most of the status updates, displaying only the most important ones. To deem what's most important, Facebook considers numerous factors, including the number of friends commenting on a certain post, how often you seem to interact with each friend, and the type of content (photo, video, status update, or link).

To view every single status update from every one of your friends, which can get pretty cluttered and difficult to follow, click **Most Recent** (above your News Feed and off to the right).

As your community of friends grows, assuming they're fairly active on Facebook, that News Feed can become very cluttered, even when you're viewing only the top news. The information you really want to see can easily get buried in a barrage of status updates, photos, videos, links, and events.

Fortunately, you can select the type of content you want to view by clicking the desired option in the left menu. Click any of the following options to reduce the clutter:

- **Welcome:** This option displays a page offering to step you through the process of getting started on Facebook. If this seems like déjà vu all over again, it is, but if you feel like you missed something the first time around, you can get a fresh start here.

- **News Feed:** This is your ticket back to the News Feed, just in case you wandered off and want to return.

- **Messages:** Click **Messages** to check your inbox for any messages your friends or other Facebook members have sent you. See Chapter 6 for details.

- **Events:** If you registered for any events or scheduled events of your own, you can click **Events** to display a list of events along with any recent news or updates relating to them. For more about the Events feature, check out Chapter 11.

- **Friends:** Clicking **Friends** displays a page that enables you to manage your Facebook friends. At the very top of the page are any friend requests you've received and haven't yet responded to. The rest of the page contains several sections devoted to helping you find friends. See Chapter 4 to find out more about connecting with people you know on Facebook.

Click **Top News** to focus
on the most important updates

Click **Most Recent** to view
all status updates as they're posted

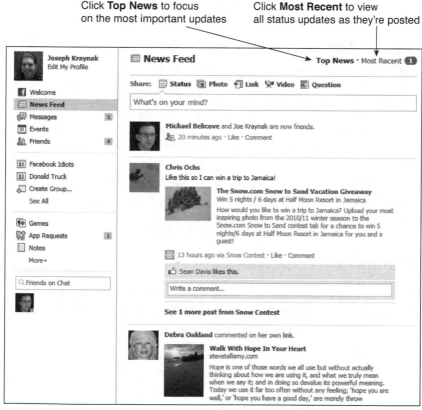

You can view all posts listed from newest to oldest or focus on the top news.

The items at the top of the left menu are Facebook's core features. The left menu also contains a list of any groups you belong to, a Create Group option for creating your own group, and a list of popular applications called *Facebook apps*. Click the **More** link below the short list of Facebook apps to expand the list. You can click items in this list to view status updates related to those apps. For example, if you want your News Feed to display only photos your friends have recently posted, click **Photos**. To find out which groups they belong to, click **Groups**.

Checking Out Your Wall

If "good fences make good neighbors," Walls on Facebook make the best of friends. On Facebook, Walls aren't used to wall in or wall out. They're used to communicate, sort of like a graffiti artist uses walls as his canvas to broadcast messages.

WHOA!

Communicating via Walls reduces the frenetic clutter of status updates characteristic of the News Feed, but Wall-to-Wall discussions are not private. Anyone who can access your Wall or your friend's Wall can read the content of your posts, and some Wall posts may show up in your mutual friends' News Feeds. You can restrict access to your Wall by adjusting your privacy settings, as discussed in Chapter 2.

In the following sections, you find out how to access your Wall and your friends' Walls, configure your Wall, and use Walls to carry on more direct conversations with a friend.

Heading to Your Wall

Your Wall is your own space on Facebook. It's what your friends see when they click your name or photo. It's also what you see when you click your name or photo or click **Profile** in the top menu.

Your Wall displays your status updates and content that friends have posted to your Wall.

Bumping Into a Friend's Wall

Except for the content posted on a friend's Wall, it looks almost identical to your own Wall and contains many of the same features, though they may be called something different. Another difference is that your friend's Wall has a Message and Poke button (upper right), so you can communicate privately with your friend.

You can send a message to or poke a friend.

Posting to Your Wall or News Feed

At the top of the News Feed and the Wall is Facebook's Publisher. Its primary purpose is to enable you to post text informing your friends of what you're doing, planning to do, thinking, or feeling at this very moment. It's very similar to posting a "tweet" on Twitter— something referred to as *microblogging.* You use the Publisher to post status updates (also called stories) and other content to your News Feed or Wall or to a friend's Wall.

Adding a post to your News Feed or Wall is one of the easiest things to do on Facebook; follow these steps:

1. Click **Home** or **Profile** (in the top menu) to post in your News Feed or on your Wall. Either way, what you post will appear in both your News Feed and on your Wall. (Click a friend to post the update to your friend's Wall, addressing the post more directly to this particular friend.)

2. Click in the **What's on your mind?** box and type your message.

3. (Optional) Click any of the controls near the What's on your mind? box to add a question, photo, link, or video, as explained in the following sections.

4. (Optional) Click the privacy button (the button with the lock on it below and toward the right of where you typed your message) and click the desired privacy option:

   • **Everyone:** All Facebook members can read your post.

   • **Friends of Friends:** Only your Facebook friends and their friends can read your post.

   • **Only Friends:** Only your Facebook friends can read the post. (This is the default setting.)

   • **Customize:** Displays the Custom Privacy dialog box that provides additional control over who can read your post. If you have one or more friend lists, this comes in very handy for sharing a post with a select group of friends.

5. Click **Share**. Facebook displays the update in the News Feed or on the Wall where you posted it.

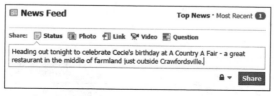

Post a status update to keep your friends informed about what you're up to.

Posting a Question

A great way to solicit feedback from friends is to post a question. Facebook enables you to post only the question or post the question along with poll options to keep a running tally of what your friends think, such as whether you should change careers, start dating a certain someone, or which movie you should rent.

WHOA!

Don't ask a question you don't want people other than your Facebook friends to read. When you post a question, your friends might share the question with their friends, who might share it with their friends, and so on. This can be a good thing if you want lots of feedback, but a bad thing if you didn't plan to share it with the world.

To post a question, click **Question** near the What's on your mind? box and the box changes to Ask something .... Click in that box and type your question. If you want to poll your friends, click the **Add Poll Options** link and type your options in the resulting text boxes. To restrict the choices to the items you typed, deselect the option **Allow anyone to add options**. When you're ready to post the question, click **Ask Question**.

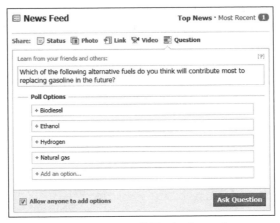

Ask a question or poll Facebook members.

Attaching a Photo

Most people love viewing photos, particularly interesting photos of people they know and love, so consider including an occasional photo in your status updates. All you need to do is click the Photo icon near the Status box and follow the on-screen cues and instructions prior to sharing your update. When you click Photo, Facebook presents the following options:

- **Upload a Photo:** Click **Upload a Photo**, click **Browse**, select a photo stored on your computer, click **Open**, and Facebook uploads the photo for you.

- **Take a Photo:** Assuming your computer is equipped with a functioning webcam, click **Take a Photo**, click the little camera icon near the bottom of the photo preview area, give your permission to access the camera if prompted, strike a pose, and wait for Facebook to snap your picture. After you click the camera icon, a three-second on-screen countdown commences. When the camera icon reappears, Facebook is done snapping your mug shot or whatever you're holding up to the camera. If you don't like the photo, click the **X** in the upper right of the photo and do your reshoot.

- **Create an Album:** Click **Create an Album** and follow the on-screen instructions to upload photos and create your album.

Facebook prompts you to upload a photo, take a photo with your webcam, or create a new photo album.

FRIEND-LY ADVICE

You can upload photos via e-mail! After clicking **Attach Photos > Upload a Photo**, click the **upload via email** link to obtain a special e-mail address where you can send photos to have them uploaded to Facebook. When you upload a photo via e-mail, it's posted to your News Feed as a status update and is visible to all of your friends. The subject line becomes the photo's caption. (In Chapter 7, you learn how to create albums and enter settings that enable you to control where your e-mail uploaded photos are posted and who can view them.)

Attaching a Video

Everyone loves a good video, so if you're handy with a digital cam-corder or love to record cameo appearances with your webcam, you can easily upload your clips or record them directly to Facebook and include them with your status updates.

Keep in mind that Facebook's policies restrict members to posting only videos they or their friends have made. If you want to include a video from somewhere else on the Internet, insert a link to it, as explained later in this chapter.

To post a video, click **Video**, click one of the following options, and follow the on-screen cues and instructions to record or upload the video clip you want to attach:

- **Record a Video:** To record a video using your webcam, click **Record a Video**, give your permission to access the camera if prompted, click the little red dot near the bottom of the photo preview area, wait for Facebook to start recording, and then do your thing. When you're done, click the red but-ton again to stop recording. If you don't like the video, click the **X** in the upper right of the video and repeat the steps to "Take two!"

- **Upload a Video:** If you already have a video clip stored on your computer, click **Upload a Video**, click **Browse**, select a video file stored on your computer, click **Open**, and Facebook will upload the video for you. This can take some time, depending on the size of the file and your connection speed.

Inserting a Link

To call attention to web content outside your News Feed, you can easily post a link to it. Your friends can then click the link to check out the web page for themselves.

Before you share a link, make sure you have the right address of the page you want to link to. Open that page in your browser window, click in the **Address** box to highlight the page's address, and then press the keystroke you use to copy stuff. You can now share the link.

Near the Status box, click **Link**. The Link form appears. Click in the **http://** box and type or paste the web page address you copied. (You don't need to type http:// at the beginning of the address.) Click **Attach**. Facebook attaches the link along with a portion of the first sentence from the source page. If the page contains photos or images, you'll be prompted to select a thumbnail image representative of the link. Use the arrow buttons to select the thumbnail you want, or click **No Thumbnail**. Type something in the text box if you want to, then click **Share**.

You can link to web pages from the Publisher.

Adding Other Stuff

In addition to photos, videos, events, and links, Facebook allows you to attach and post other stuff, depending on the applications you use. To attach other items, click the **More** button (if available), choose the item you want to attach, and enter any required settings as prompted.

Keep in mind that what's listed in the More menu is limited to standard Facebook applications and other Facebook applications you've used. If you've used only a few Facebook apps, you may not see a More button. For more about Facebook applications, see Part 3.

Responding to a Friend's Post

When a friend posts something to his Wall or News Feed, it typically appears in your News Feed, unless your friend kept you out of the loop. You can then read the update, post a comment on it, "like" it (give it the thumbs up), and even share the update with your other friends.

Posting a Comment

The most common response to a friend's status update, other than ignoring it completely or just reading it, is to comment on it. Click in the **Write a comment ...** box just below the message, type your comment, and press **Enter** to post your comment. (If the Write a comment ... box isn't visible, you might need to click the **Comment** link that appears near your friend's status update.)

WHOA!

Whatever you write as a comment will be viewable by all of your friend's Facebook friends as well as all your friends. If your comment is of a highly personal nature, take a minute to think it through before commenting in public, and consider sending your thoughts with a Facebook message instead. See Chapter 6 for more about Facebook's Message feature.

You can easily comment on a friend's post.

Voting Your Approval

Even easier than posting a comment is to express your approval of what your friend posted. All you need to do is click the **Like** link just below the post. A little thumbs-up icon appears, along with your username, indicating your vote of approval. Another way to respond to a friend's post is to share it with your friends by posting it to your News Feed or sending it via a message to one or more friends. Click the **Share** link below the post. (The Share link appears only if your friend's privacy settings allow friends to share.) Type a brief message introducing the item you're reposting and indicating why you think it's noteworthy. To repost the item, click **Share**. To send it as a message, click **Send as a Message instead** (lower left) and then click the **Send Message** button.

Hiding a Friend's Status Updates

When a friend is monopolizing the conversation on your Wall or News Feed by posting too much content that doesn't really interest you, you can easily hide that person's posts:

1. Rest the mouse pointer on a post from the friend whose updates you want to hide, and click the **X** (to the right of the post's title).

2. Click **Hide this post** or **Hide all by** followed by your friend's name. Poof! The status update or all status updates this friend posted magically disappear from your News Feed and Wall.

You can hide a friend's status updates.

To hide something other than a status update, such as a game that one or more of your friends likes to play, hover the mouse pointer over any post that contains the content you want to hide, click **X** (to the right of the post's title), and then click **Hide** followed by the content you want to hide, such as **Hide FarmVille**.

You can unhide posts and content you've chosen to hide. To show a single post you've hidden, click **Undo** next to the post, if the Undo option is available. To show all posts from someone you've hidden, scroll to the bottom of the News Feed and click **Edit Options**. The Edit Your News Feed Settings dialog box appears. Click the **X** next to the friend whose posts you want to display in your News Feed and click **Save**. Facebook refreshes your News Feed to display the previously hidden posts.

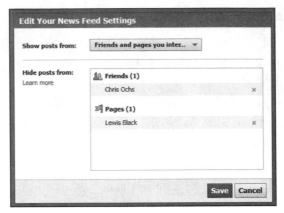

You can add hidden content back into your News Feed.

Posting to a Friend's Wall

Assuming your friend allows friends to post to her Wall and hasn't specifically blocked you from doing so, you can write on your friend's Wall by posting a message or comment. Whatever you post can be seen not only by your friend but also by any of your friend's friends. It will also appear in your mutual friends' News Feeds.

To post to your friend's Wall, first head there by clicking your friend's name or photo. You can then proceed to do one of the following:

- Click in the **Write something ...** box, type your message, attach something if you like, and click **Share**.

- Click the **Comment** link below any of your friend's posts, type a comment, and click **Comment**.

Connecting One-on-One via a Friendship Page

As the old saying goes, "Two's company. Three's a crowd." Fortunately, Facebook enables you to focus on your one-to-one relationships free of the usual clutter on your Wall or News Feed. Whenever you post to a friend's Wall or your friend posts to your Wall, the post appears with another link after it: See Friendship. Click the **See Friendship** link.

This takes you to your friendship page with this particular friend, where you can engage in one-on-one discussions. Everything your friend posts on your Wall, including comments to your posts, appear on this friendship page that the two of you can access. This doesn't mean, however, that your conversations between one another are necessarily private. Your other friends may be able to check out the conversations depending on your privacy settings.

Your friendship page gives you a virtual snapshot of your Facebook friendship, displaying Wall posts you've exchanged, mutual friends, events you've both attended, photos you're both tagged in, and things you both "like."

You can follow discussions between friends.

If the discussion doesn't include you, you can still comment on or "like" one of your friend's status updates, but you can't post a comment of your own. If you're involved in the discussion, you can post a comment or a follow-up post, which then appears on the friendship page.

If two of your friends have shared something with one another, you may be able to see what they've shared via their friendship page, assuming neither friend prohibits access via their privacy settings. If two friends are exchanging Wall posts, for example, you can click **See Friendship** below a Wall post between the two friends.

POKE

You can access a friendship page at any time. Head to your friend's Wall and click the **See Friendship** link (upper right last we checked).

Wishing a Friend a Happy Birthday

Most people, unless they're hard-core curmudgeons or would rather be dead, appreciate receiving a birthday note, so if a friend's birthday is coming up, consider wishing them a happy birthday on Facebook. Facebook will even remind you! Even though it has over hundreds of millions of users, Facebook does a spectacular job of keeping track of everyone's birthday. In the column to the right of your News Feed, Facebook displays reminders of any of your friends' birthdays that are coming up soon.

To receive advance notification of upcoming friend's birthdays via e-mail, click **Account** in the top menu and then **Account Settings**. On the Account Settings page, click the **Notifications** tab, and under Facebook, select the e-mail option for "Has a birthday coming up." Each week you'll receive a concise e-mail from Facebook with information about your friends' upcoming birthdays.

Poking a Friend

On Facebook, you can poke or be poked. When you poke a friend, you're letting the person know you're thinking of her. She can then poke you back or simply ignore you.

To poke a friend, head to the person's Wall by clicking on his name or Profile image, and then click the **Poke** button (upper right). This sends a Poke notification to your friend's Home page with the options to Poke Back or click the **X** next to the poke to remove it.

If someone is poking you incessantly and won't stop even after you ask them to, you can block the person, as explained in Chapter 2. You can disable poking notifications that show up in your e-mail Inbox on the Notifications tab in Account Settings.

Liking and Sharing Stuff

Sprinkled throughout Facebook and all over the web are links that enable you to share content with your friends on Facebook or "like" it:

- **Like:** When you click **Like**, Facebook immediately posts a link to the content to your Profile, so it shows up on your Wall and in your News Feed.

- **Share:** When you click **Share**, Facebook displays the Post to Profile box, so you can add a description or a brief explanation of why you think your friends will find it relevant. Share also provides the option of sharing privately with one or more friends via a message, instead of posting it publicly to your Profile.

You're likely to see the Facebook Share or Like icon in all sorts of places—on web pages, blog posts, photo sites, video sites, and so on. From within Facebook, you can share or like your and your friends' photos, videos, notes, and anything else containing the Share or Like icons.

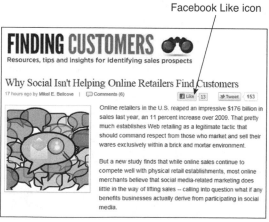

Facebook Like icon

The Facebook Like icon is popping up on sites all over the web.

On some sites, you might see a different type of share icon that doesn't look like the Facebook Like or Share link, but it still enables you to share on Facebook. If you see a generic share icon, try clicking it. It may open a menu that provides options for sharing the content on Facebook, Twitter, MySpace, and other social networks. You can proceed by clicking the option to share the item on Facebook.

After you click the option to share on Facebook, you're automatically transported to Facebook, where you can log in (if you're not already logged in) and complete the Post to Profile box. Type a message introducing the content you're about to share, then click the **Share** button.

WHOA!

Share with care. You can seriously damage or destroy a relationship by sharing content that a friend strongly disagrees with, finds offensive, or had no intention of sharing with others. When choosing material to share, consider avoiding hot-button issues like politics or religion. And never, ever pass along sensitive information that your friend shared with you in confidence. If you have any doubt about sharing something a friend posted, ask your friend before sharing it with others.

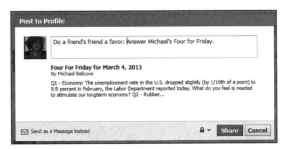

You can share a friend's post by posting it to your Profile, which places it on your Wall and in your News Feed.

The Least You Need to Know

- Your News Feed contains status updates and notifications of your friends' activities on Facebook. Your Wall contains a running display of your status updates along with comments and content added by friends and a list of your activities on Facebook.

- Posting a status update is easy. Click **What's on your mind?** in the Publisher and share away.

- You can post photos and videos by clicking on the appropriate icon in the bottom part of the Publisher.

- To comment on a friend's post, click the **Comment** link below the post or click in the **Write a comment** box, type your comment, and press **Enter**.

- To share or "like" content on or outside of Facebook, click the Facebook **Share** or **Like** icon or link: Like posts the content immediately to your Profile, whereas Share displays the post to your Profile box so you can add some commentary or share it via a message.

Communicating with Facebook Messaging

In This Chapter

- Conversing via messages, texting, chat, and Facebook e-mail
- Exchanging messages with your friends
- Searching for specific messages and conversations
- Checking out your Facebook notifications

Facebook's Messages feature has always functioned as an internal e-mail system for Facebook members, enabling them to conduct conversations in private. However, in 2011, Facebook completely revamped Messages to include multiple forms of private communication, including messages, chats, texts, and e-mail (assuming you choose to create an @facebook.com e-mail address). This enables you to pull up a conversation with someone and view a complete history of your interactions on and off Facebook. You can even loop new people into a conversation and leave a conversation that no longer interests you. This chapter shows you how.

Activating E-Mail, Texting, and Chat

Head to your Home page and click **Messages** (in the left menu). Regardless of whether you have any messages, you should see a bar just above the Messages area that includes three steps to fully access Facebook's Messages feature. You don't need to perform all three steps. Activate only the features you want to use.

- **Facebook email:** You can claim your Facebook e-mail address of yourname@facebook.com so Facebook can help you track your e-mail exchanges that occur outside the confines of Facebook. To activate Facebook e-mail, click **Claim your Facebook email**, use the resulting box to choose your e-mail address, and click **Activate Email**.

- **Text messaging:** To enable your Facebook friends to send text messages to your mobile device, click **Turn on text messaging**, use the resulting box to choose your country and mobile carrier, click **Next**, and follow the on-screen cues to complete the operation. (See Chapter 15 for more about Facebook Mobile.)

- **Facebook Chat:** If you chose to go offline with Facebook Chat (see Chapter 10), you can click **Go online to chat** so your friends can converse with you via Chat and Facebook can log your conversations as messages.

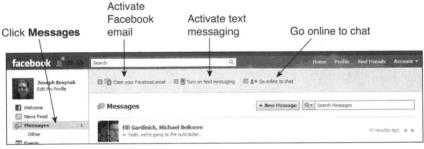

Activate the features you want to use.

Accessing Messages

Whenever you log in to Facebook, the top menu shows the number of messages you've received but haven't yet read (if any). To view a list of recent messages, click the **Messages** icon. The Messages menu drops down, displaying several of your most recent messages with the newest message first.

To get to your Messages page, click **See All Messages** (at the bottom of the menu) or, from your Home page, click **Messages** (left menu).

This takes you to a list of all messages you received—both those you have and haven't read. Unread messages are shaded a light blue and have a dark blue dot next to them; those you've already read are unshaded with a circle next to them. If you have more than one screen of messages, you can click the forward and back buttons below the list to view the next or previous screen.

The Messages icon   Your messages

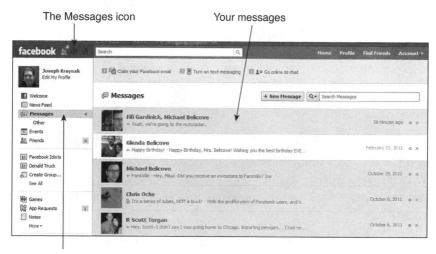

Click **Messages**

Your Messages area displays a list of messages you received.

Reading and Replying to New Messages

To read a message, click it. The contents of the message appear. To reply to a message, click in the text box below the message, type your reply, and press **Enter**. In addition to replying with text, you can attach a file, photo, or video by clicking the relevant icon below the message box.

Below and to the right of the message box are a couple more options. The first one enables you to text the message to the person's cell phone as well as send it on Facebook. The second option toggles Quick Reply mode. When Quick Reply is on, you type your message and press **Enter** to send it. When Quick Reply is off, you type your message and then click the **Reply** or **Reply All** button to send it. (If Quick Reply is off, pressing **Enter** starts a new paragraph.)

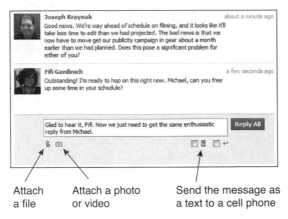

Attach   Attach a photo   Send the message as
a file   or video   a text to a cell phone

The message appears and you can reply to it.

If you received a message and replied to it, or you sent a message and the recipient replied, both the original message and response are shown together; that way, you can follow the discussion thread without having to search for old messages to see what you or someone else said.

You can always return to the list of messages by clicking **Messages** in the left menu or the **< Messages** button above the conversation.

Adding Someone to the Conversation

When you need to bring someone else into the loop, you can add the person to the conversation. First, display the conversation on its own page. Then, click **Actions** (top right) **> Add People ....** The Add People box appears. Click in the **Enter a friend's name** box, start typing a friend's name, and when you see the name you want, click it. You can add more friends by continuing to type and click names. When you're done, click **Add People**.

A message appears inside the conversation listing the people you've added the conversation. Now, when anyone in the conversation replies to all, the people you've brought into the loop will receive the reply.

Leaving the Conversation

Whether you started the conversation or one of your friends included you in it, you can always leave. Open the conversation on its own page, click the **Actions** button, and click **Leave Conversation**. When Facebook prompts you for confirmation, click **Leave Conversation**.

Forwarding a Message

You can forward one or more messages in a conversation or the entire conversation to another friend. First, open the conversation on its own page. Then, click **Actions** (upper right) **> Forward**. Click each message you want to forward so a checkmark appears next to it, and then click **Forward**. The Forward Message box appears.

Click in the **To** box and start typing the future recipient's name or e-mail address. As you start to type, Facebook displays the names of your Facebook friends that match what you've typed so far. If you see the desired name, click it. If not, keep typing. You can add more names and e-mail addresses if you'd like to forward the message to additional recipients.

Click in the **Message** box, type an explanation of why you're forwarding the message, and then click the **Send** button.

Searching for Messages

Given that Facebook gathers messages from a variety of sources, you can expect your inbox to become quite cluttered. To help you sort through the mounds of messages, Facebook includes a search tool.

You can search for messages by name (sender or recipient) or by keyword (to find all messages that mention the upcoming family reunion, for example). To search for a message, click in the **Search Messages** box, type a friend's name or a keyword or phrase, and press **Enter**.

FRIEND-LY ADVICE

If you're typing a friend's name, you usually need to type only the first few letters. Facebook auto-completes the entry for you.

Facebook displays a list of all the messages that match your search entry. You can then click the message you want to read.

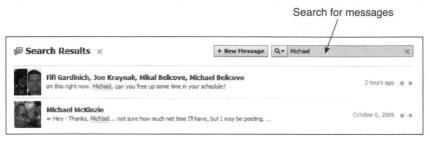

You can search for messages by name or keyword.

You can also filter the list of messages to show only Unread, Archived, or Sent messages or those you've sent and received using your Facebook e-mail address. To filter messages, click the magnifying glass icon to the left of the Search Messages box and click the desired option: Unread Messages, Archived Messages, Sent Messages, or Email Only.

Flagging Messages as Unread

As you open messages, presumably to read them, Facebook marks them as "read." This means the message no longer appears in the count of new messages that Facebook displays next to the Messages icon in the top menu. It also means you can open the Search menu and click **Unread Messages** above the message list to filter out messages you've already read.

If a message is important, you may want to flag it as unread after reading it, so it doesn't get lost in the list. To flag a single message as unread, click the circle (to the right of the message, last we checked). The circle turns into a dot. To mark a message as read, click the dot to turn it into a circle. When you rest the mouse pointer on the circle or dot, Mark as Read or Mark as Unread appears, so you can tell whether you're about to mark the message as read or unread.

If you're viewing a message by itself (not in the list of messages), an Actions button appears above the message. To mark the message as unread, click **Actions** and then **Mark as Unread**.

Archiving or Deleting a Message

When you're done with a particular message or discussion, you can archive or delete it. If you're viewing a list of messages, you can only archive (not delete) messages from the list. (Archiving removes the message from the list but stores it in the archives so you can get it back later.) To archive a message, click the **X** (to the right of the message last we checked).

If you're viewing a message on its own page, you can archive or delete it. Click the **Actions** button (above and to the right of the conversation) and click the desired action: **Archive** or **Delete Messages**. If you choose to delete messages, a checkbox appears next to each message in the conversation. You can click the checkbox next to each message you want to delete and then click **Delete Selected** or click **Delete All** to delete the entire conversation.

> **WHOA!**
>
> Deleting a thread (discussion) deletes all messages in that discussion—so before you click that Delete button, make sure you really want everything in that thread deleted.

Reporting Spam

Facebook's setup is not prone to spam, but spammers are known to bend and break the rules. As a result, you may become the unfortunate recipient of Facebook e-mail spam. If you do receive spam, report it to Facebook so management can crack down on the perpetrators.

To report spam, select the spam message or conversation, click the **Actions** button (above and to the right of the conversation), and click **Report as Spam**. The Report as Spam? dialog box appears prompting you for confirmation. Click **Report as Spam**.

Outgoing! Sending Messages

Usually, you have to send mail to get mail, so if you want a Messages list brimming with messages from your Facebook friends, start composing and sending messages. In the following sections, we show you how to compose a new message to send to an individual or to multiple recipients, whether the person is your Facebook friend or not.

Sending a New Message to a Facebook Member

Composing and sending a message in Facebook is a snap. Click the **Messages** icon in the top menu and click **Send a New Message** or, if the Messages screen is already displayed, click **+ New Message** (upper right). The New Message dialog box appears.

Now do the same thing you usually do when sending e-mail: address the message in the To box, type a message in the Message box, and click **Send**. When addressing your message, instead of typing an e-mail address, click in the **To** box and type a friend's name. (As you start typing, Facebook displays the names of friends that match what you typed so far. You can click a name to add it to the To box.)

Prior to sending the message, you can click the paperclip icon to attach a file or click the camera icon to take a photo or video of yourself (using your webcam) to attach to the outgoing message. You may also want to click the checkbox below and to the right of the Message box to text a copy of the message to the person's mobile device. (See Chapters 7 and 8 for more about pictures and video and Chapter 15 for more about Facebook Mobile.)

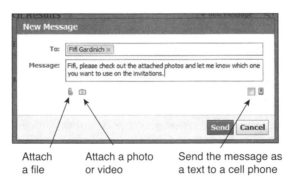

Send a message.

You can usually contact a person via Facebook messaging through the person's Profile, even if the individual isn't a Facebook friend. To do so, go to the person's Profile and click the **Message** button (upper right). Complete the message form and click **Send**.

POKE

If you're wondering where the Subject box is, Facebook has omitted it intentionally to make messages appear more conversational and less like traditional e-mail. If someone sends you an e-mail message that includes a subject line, the subject line appears in bold as the first line of the message.

Sending a Message to an Address Outside Facebook

You can send messages to e-mail addresses outside Facebook, regardless of whether the recipient is a Facebook member, by typing the person's e-mail address, instead of a friend's name, into the **To** box. Before you e-mail outside Facebook, note the following:

- Non-Facebook members can receive your messages, but they can respond to your message only if you have a Facebook e-mail address. Otherwise, to reply, they must click a link inside the message that opens a Facebook Page and prompts the person to join Facebook.

- Don't spam from Facebook. If someone complains, Facebook might cancel your account.

Mass Mailing to Multiple Recipients

You can send the same message to several recipients with a single click of a button by entering a friend list or multiple friends' names and/or e-mail addresses in the **To** box. (See Chapter 4 for instructions on how to create a friend list.)

WHOA!

Be careful when replying. Facebook members have been known to mistakenly send a reply to the entire group, thinking they were replying only to a particular individual. If the message contains something embarrassing or insulting to one or more group members you thought you were excluding, you could have a lot of explaining to do and apologies to make.

The tricky part is when you're carrying on an e-mail discussion with multiple friends. If someone replies to your message and sends the reply to the entire group, you have the option of replying to the entire group or to that particular individual. Here's what you do:

- To reply to the group, type your message in the **Reply** box and click the **Reply** button.

- To reply to the individual only, click the person's name or e-mail address, type your message in the **Reply** box, and click the **Reply** button. This creates a branched thread in which you and the other person can carry on a discussion outside the main discussion.

Taking Notice of Notifications

Unless you specify otherwise (via your account settings, as explained in Chapter 1), you will receive notifications whenever anything notable occurs on Facebook that involves you—whenever someone sends you a message, adds you as a friend, confirms your friend request, tags you in a photo, tags one of your photos, invites you to join a group, and so on.

To view recent notifications, click the **Notifications** icon (left end of the top menu). To view all Notifications, click the **Notifications** icon and then click **See All Notifications**. Each notification contains one or more links you can click to jump to the area where the activity took place or to the Profile of the person responsible. Separate links may appear so close together that they look like a single link; mouse over the link(s), and it'll be clear whether you're dealing with one or more.

Facebook also forwards the notification to the e-mail address you used to register on Facebook (unless you have modified the setting), to your instant messaging account, and/or to your cell phone or other mobile device if you're using Facebook Mobile (see Chapter 15). To subscribe to notifications via text message or RSS feed, click the **Notifications** icon, click **See All Notifications**, and then use the Subscribe links to set up your subscription(s). If you choose to subscribe via RSS feed, Facebook displays your notifications feed page. Click the **Subscribe to this feed** link and follow the instructions to add the feed to your web browser.

> **FRIEND-LY ADVICE**
>
> An RSS (Really Simple Syndication) is a technology that automatically pulls together entries and displays them on a web-based or desktop RSS reader for quick access.

The Least You Need to Know

- To access Facebook's messaging platform from your Home page, click **Messages** in the left menu or click the **Messages** icon (top menu) and then click **See All Messages**.

- To send a message, click the **Messages** icon (top menu) and then click **Send a New Message** or click the **+ New Message** button on the Messages screen and do the usual e-mail thing.

- You can send messages to people who are not Facebook members by typing their e-mail address into the **To** box.

- Click the paperclip or camera icon at the bottom of the New Message dialog box to attach a file (paperclip icon) or a photo or video (camera icon) to an outgoing message.

- To send the same message to several Facebook friends, type each friend's name into the **To** field in the New Message dialog box.

Getting More Involved with Facebook

Although you establish and maintain relationships through Facebook, you also have a relationship with Facebook that develops over time as you get to know one another. The more Facebook knows about you and your friends, the better able it is to suggest new friends and present you with more relevant information. The more you know about Facebook, the better equipped you are to tap its full potential.

When you're ready to take your relationship with Facebook to the next level, we're ready to ramp you up. Here, we introduce you to one of the most popular features on Facebook—photo sharing—along with other features you may want to explore, including video sharing, Groups, Chat, Events, Messages, and Notes. All of these features can enhance your experience on Facebook and the relationships you have with your Facebook friends.

Uploading and Sharing Photos

In This Chapter

- Viewing other people's photos
- Making photo albums to organize your photos
- Uploading quality photos on Facebook
- Tagging yourself and your friends in photos
- Limiting access to specific albums

Swapping photos online has become a favorite global pastime. With online photo-sharing services including Photobucket and Flickr, people can upload their photos and share them with anyone in the world who has a computer with Internet access.

Well, Facebook is in the photo-sharing business, too. All you have to do is create a photo album, upload your photos, and start sharing. This chapter shows you how and provides additional guidance on restricting photo access to only those people you want looking at them.

Looking at Photos

Chances are pretty good that if you've spent more than two minutes on Facebook, you've already seen a few photos. They show up in the following places:

- **News Feed:** If a friend posts a photo, a thumbnail version of it appears. You can click the photo to view a larger version and access any other photos in that album.

- **Your Profile:** Click **Profile** in the top menu and then click the **Photos** tab in the left column to check out your own photos.

- **Photostream:** Near the top of each Facebook member's Profile page is a strip of photos that person has recently been tagged in. This Photostream initially contains your Profile photos. For more about tagging photos, skip ahead to the section titled "Tagging Photos."

- **Your friends' Profiles:** Click a friend's name or Profile photo and then click the **Photos** tab to check out your friend's photos.

- **Groups:** If you belong to any Facebook groups, as explained in Chapter 9, you can view photos that group members have posted.

- **Photo application:** On your Home page, in the left menu, click **Photos**. On the Photos page that appears you can view albums your friends have recently created or updated, photos uploaded using a mobile device, photos in which your friends have been tagged, your photos, and photos of you. Using the Photos application, you can also create your own albums, as explained in the following section.

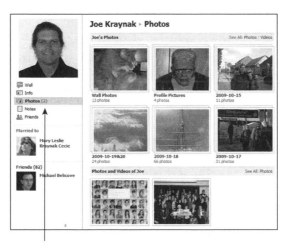

Click **Photos**

You can access a friend's photos through his Profile.

POKE

Neither Photobucket nor Flickr can claim the top spot in the online photo-sharing arena. Facebook is the champ with more than 3 billion photos uploaded to the site each month.

Preparing Photos for Uploading

After you've created an album, you can immediately begin upload-ing photos from your computer to the new album, but don't rush the process. First, make sure those photos are quality snapshots, and then organize them into folders on your computer to simplify the upload process. The following sections show you how to properly prepare your photos for upload.

Editing Your Photos: Quality Counts

Too many Facebook members focus, snap, and upload—often skimp-ing on the "focus" part. As a result, their albums are cluttered with lousy snapshots—too dark, too light, too much glare, weird colors, and so on. Prior to uploading your photos, use a photo-editing pro-gram to make them look as good as they possibly can be.

Most digital cameras and many printers come with their own photo-editing software. If you have no such program on your computer, consider first uploading the photos to a photo-sharing service, such as Flickr (www.flickr.com), that has photo-editing tools. You can then import your photos into Facebook as explained later in this chapter. Google's Picasa (www.picasa.google.com) is another option. With Picasa, you edit the photos on your computer and then upload them to Picasa to share them. With a Picasa Facebook app, you can even upload your photos to Facebook right after editing them. We cover Flickr and Picasa near the end of this chapter.

Edit your photos to ensure quality.

Organizing Photos into Folders

Whenever you *download* photos from your camera to your computer, you should store the photos in separate folders. Each folder can function as a separate album. This enables you to quickly upload an entire folder full of photos from your computer to one of your Facebook albums without having to select individual photos to include or exclude.

If you haven't organized the photos on your computer in separate folders, take some time and organize them now. We'll wait.

Uploading Photos

To make photos available on Facebook, you need to upload (copy) them from your computer or mobile device to Facebook. As with most tasks, Facebook offers more than one way to upload photos. In addition, you can use third-party applications that some Facebook members find faster and more convenient. In the following sections, you get to check out the various methods and choose the one you like best.

> **POKE**
>
> *Uploading* and *downloading* are fancy words for *copying*. The direction, up or down, is relative to you. If you're copying something from somewhere else to the device you're using, you're downloading. If you're copying from the device you're using to somewhere else, you're uploading.

Uploading Photos to a New Album

To upload your photos to a new photo album using Facebook's Photo Uploader, here's what you do:

1. From your Home or Profile page, click **Photos** (left menu).

2. Click **+ Upload Photos** (upper right). The Upload Photos box appears prompting you to select photos.

3. Click **Select Photos**. The Select Files to Upload dialog box appears.

4. Select the folder (on your computer) where the photos are stored. Facebook displays thumbnail versions of the photos in the selected folder.

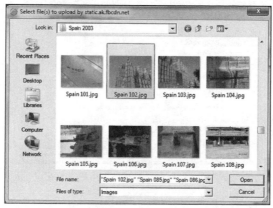

Select the photos you want to upload.

5. Select the photos you want to upload just as you would select files on your computer.

6. Click the **Open** button. Upload Photos dialog box appears and starts uploading the photos. This may take several minutes depending on the number of photos, their size and quality, and the speed of your Internet connection.

7. Highlight the entry in the **Name of album** box and type a descriptive name for the album.

8. (Optional) Click in the **Location** box and type the location where the photos were taken.

9. To include high-resolution photos, click the **High Resolution** option.

10. Open the **Share album with list** and click the option that describes which friends, if any, you want to share the album with: **Everyone**, **Friends of Friends**, **Friends Only**, or **Custom**. If you choose Custom, use the resulting screen to enter your preferences.

11. Click **Create Album**. Facebook creates a new album for the photos you just uploaded and prompts you to tag any people in the photos. For more about tagging photos, see "Tagging Photos," later in this chapter.

Create an album in which to store this set of photos.

Uploading Photos to an Existing Album

If you already have a photo album and want to add more photos to it, click **Profile** and then click the **Photos** tab. Click the album into which you want to upload more photos, and then click the **Add Photos** button (upper right). This starts Facebook's Photos Uploader, which you can use to upload additional photos as explained in the previous section starting with step 3. The process is a little less involved because you're not creating a new album.

To find out how to upload photos from your cell phone or other mobile device, head to Chapter 15.

Editing Your Photos and Albums

After uploading photos to an album on Facebook, you can edit the album or the photos it contains to add information about each photo, rearrange the photos in the album, delete photos, and more.

To get started, click **Profile**, click your **Photos** tab, click the album you want to work with, and click the **Edit Album** link just above the photos. The Edit Album dialog box appears, enabling you to change the album name, add a location and description, and change the privacy setting for the album. This dialog box also provides links to edit photos in the album and delete the album.

Edit information and
privacy settings for
the album

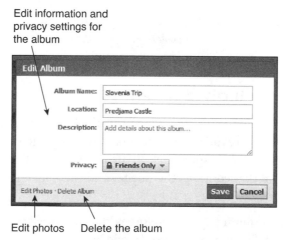

Edit photos   Delete the album

You can customize the album, edit its photos, or delete it.

If you click the **Edit Photos** link, the Edit Album page appears, displaying a list of photos in the album. For each photo, you have the option to add a description, tag people in the photo, choose the photo as your album cover, delete the photo, or move the photo to a different album. The Edit Album page also contains an Edit Info tab (to edit information about the album) and a Delete tab (to delete the album and everything in it).

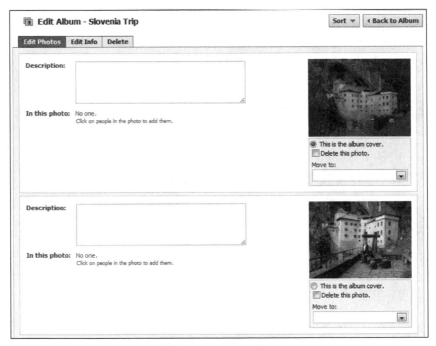

Edit photos in an album.

Working on Individual Photos

You can do a great deal of customizing in the Edit Album page, but some options are unavailable unless you view an image on its own page. To view an image solo, click **Profile**, click your **Photos** tab, click the album that contains the image, and then click the image.

In this view, you can make many of the same changes you can make using the Edit Album page, including adding a description, tagging the photo, and deleting the photo. In addition, you can take the following actions:

- **Comment on the photo.** Click in the **Write a comment** box, type your comment, and press **Enter.**

- **Rotate the photo 90 degrees clockwise or counterclockwise.** Click the **Counterclockwise Rotate** or **Clockwise Rotate** button. (These buttons look like curved arrows pointing counterclockwise and clockwise, respectively.)

- **Share the photo.** To post the photo and your comment to your Wall, click **Share**, type whatever you want to say about the photo, and click **Share**; to send it as an e-mail, click the **Send as a Message instead** link, type the name of the Facebook friend you want to send it to, type a message, and click **Send Message.**

- **Make the photo your Profile picture.** Click **Make Profile Picture.**

Tagging Photos

Facebook lets you tag photos (yours or your friends') to identify people in those photos. Anyone viewing the photo can then mouse over people shown in the photo to view the tag. Whenever you tag a photo, the action is recorded in your News Feed, so your friends will know when you've tagged yourself or one of them. If you tag one of your Facebook friends, Facebook sends the person a notification and posts it in the person's News Feed.

To tag a photo, here's what you do:

1. Display the photo you want to tag. You can display the photo on the Edit Photos tab or on its own page.

2. If you're viewing the photo on its own page, click **Tag This Photo** below and to the left of the photo. (If you're on the Edit Photos tab, you don't have the Tag This Photo option. Instead, when you mouse over the thumbnail version of the photo, the mouse pointer morphs into crosshairs and you just click whatever you want to tag in the photo.)

3. Position the mouse pointer (crosshairs) over the center of the person's face for the most accurate placement of your tag and click. The Tag box appears, in which you can do one of the following.

- Choose your Facebook friend's name from the list provided.

- Click in the **Type any name or tag** box and start typing the name of the person or object. As you type, the list of friend names narrows to match what you've typed so far, and you can click a name in the list. If you're tagging a person (or object) who isn't a Facebook friend, just finish typing the name. (You can add the person's e-mail address to invite him to join Facebook and see the photo you just tagged him in.)

4. Repeat steps 2 and 3 to tag other people and objects in the photo.

5. Click **Tag** or **Done Tagging**.

Click the person or object

Type or select a name

Tag yourself or your friends in photos.

WHOA!

Some people don't appreciate being tagged in photos, particularly if they think the photo captured them in an unflattering light or embarrassing pose, so be careful. If a friend removes a tag or requests that you remove a photo, respect her wishes. If a friend keeps tagging you in photos and you want that to stop, send your friend a message asking her to cease and desist (diplomatically, of course). If she continues, consider de-friending her so she won't be able to tag you. For more about de-friending, check out Chapter 4. One more thing: Don't even think about using tags to advertise or promote a product or service.

You can remove a tag at any time. When you display a tagged photo, the tags appear below the photo. Next to the tag you want to remove, click **Remove tag**.

Rearranging Photos in Your Album

Unless you specify otherwise, Facebook displays the photos in an album in the order in which you uploaded them. You can rearrange the photos at any time. Here's how:

1. Click **Profile** in the top menu and then click **Photos** (left menu). Your Photos page appears.

2. Click the album you want to rearrange. Facebook displays a page showing the photos in that album.

3. Drag and drop the photos to manually rearrange them.

Another way to rearrange photos is to sort them from oldest to newest or vice versa on the Edit Album page. On your Profile page, click **Photos** (on the left), click the album that contains the photos you want to rearrange, click **Edit Album**, and click the **Edit Photos** link. Click the **Sort** button (above the list of photos) and click the desired sort order: **Newest to Oldest** or **Oldest to Newest**.

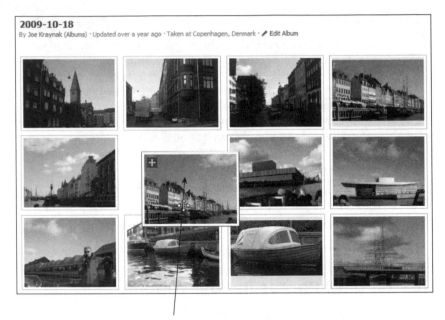

Drag and drop photos

You can rearrange the photos in an album.

Managing Your Photos with Third-Party Applications

Facebook is actually ill-equipped to handle photos. Sure, you can upload photos and share them with your friends, but Facebook lacks the file-management and photo-editing tools present in dedicated photo-management services like Flickr and Picasa. As a result, you tend to see a lot of bad photos on Facebook—photos that are too dark, too light, have red-eye issues, and so on.

Because Facebook lacks the essential photo enhancement tools, consider using a full-featured program or service and linking it to your Facebook account. Facebook includes applications for the most popular photo-sharing services, including Flickr and Picasa, which enable you to upload photos directly to Facebook. The following sections show you how.

Linking to Picasa

Google features an excellent photo-management program called *Picasa* that you can download (for free!) and use on your computer to manage your photos, edit them to look just right, and upload them into Picasa web folders (on Google). With the addition of the Picasa Uploader application for Facebook, you can edit the photos on your computer in Picasa and then upload them directly to your albums on Facebook—and even create new albums.

To learn more about Picasa and download and install your free copy of the program, visit picasa.google.com.

After installing Picasa, take the following steps to install the Picasa Uploader for Facebook:

1. Close your web browser and restart it. Otherwise, if you try to install the Picasa plugin, Facebook won't recognize your recent Picasa installation and won't allow you to continue.

2. Go to apps.facebook.com/picasauploader.

3. Click **Install Now** and follow the on-screen instructions to complete the installation. This adds a button to Picasa that allows you to upload photos directly from Picasa to Facebook.

When you're ready to upload photos from Picasa to Facebook, select the photos in Picasa as you normally do and then click the **Facebook** button. The Facebook Uploader dialog box appears. Click **Start Upload**.

Select the images
you want to upload

Click the Facebook icon

You can upload photos directly from Picasa to Facebook.

Linking to Flickr

Yahoo!'s Flickr is the most popular service dedicated exclusively to digital photo sharing. Go to www.flickr.com, register for the service (it's free), and you can instantly begin uploading your photos. (To find additional tools for enhancing your Flickr experience, including the Flickr Uploadr for your desktop, visit www.flickr.com/tools.) After you've uploaded some photos to your Flickr account, you can link your account to Facebook using an application like Flickr Importr. Here's how:

1. Go to apps.facebook.com/flickrimportr. Facebook displays a confirmation screen asking whether you want to give this application access to your information.

2. Click **Allow** and follow any additional on-screen instructions
    to complete the authentication.

After you've linked your Flickr account to your Facebook account,
you can access Flickr Importr by clicking **Flickr Importr** in the
applications section of the left menu.

> **POKE**
>
> Facebook has several applications available for importing photos from
> Flickr—and some are better than others. If Flickr Importr doesn't work
> for you, head to your Home page, click **App Requests**, scroll down past
> the Friends' Apps section, click the **Apps Directory** link, and search for
> other Flickr applications. See Chapter 13 for more about hunting down
> Facebook applications.

With Flickr Importr, you simply click **Photos** to view thumbnails of
the photos you have stored in your Flickr account. Click each photo
you want to import into Facebook, and click **Submit**. You can then
create a new Facebook album or add photos to an existing album and
enter options for each photo. When you're done entering your preferences, click **Start Import**. Flickr Importr imports the photos from
Flickr and places them in the specified album.

After importing the photos, open the album in which they're stored,
select the photos, and then click the **Approve** button. You can then
tag the photos, add descriptions, share the album, and so on.

Select the photos

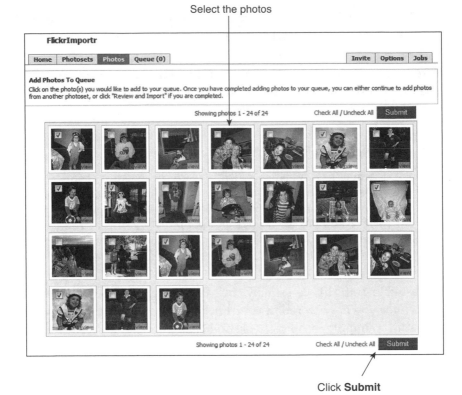

Click **Submit**

Flickr Importr can pull photos from Flickr into Facebook.

The Least You Need to Know

- To access your Photos page, click **Profile** (in the top menu) and then click your **Photos** tab.

- To create a photo album, click **Profile**, click your **Photos** tab, click **+ Upload Photos**, and follow the on-screen cues.

- To view photos in one of your albums, click **Profile**, click the **Photos** tab, and click the album.

- Click a photo in your album to display it on a page of its own. From there, you can change the description, add a comment, rotate the photo, tag people or objects shown in the photo, delete the photo, or make it your Profile photo.

- To tag yourself or a friend in a photo, click the photo to display it on its own page, click **Tag This Photo**, click the person, and then select the person's name from your friend list.

Uploading and Sharing Video Footage

In This Chapter

- Viewing your friends' video clips
- Adhering to Facebook's video guidelines
- Sharing your own video clips with friends
- Editing your video clips
- Getting personal with video e-mail

YouTube may be the leader in video hosting and sharing, but Facebook is no slouch in this arena. Members can upload video clips, post video clips on their Walls, tag and comment on clips, post notes with video, and even record footage directly to Facebook using a webcam!

Whether you're an indie filmmaker looking to spread the word about your new feature film or a proud parent wanting to share Junior's first steps with your extended family, this chapter helps you project your footage onto your Wall and share it on Facebook.

Viewing Other People's Video Clips

You don't have to fire up your camcorder to start enjoying Facebook's video features. If you have any filmmakers among your Facebook friends, you can watch their videos. In the following sections, we show you how to watch a video clip and comment on it, tag yourself or your Facebook friends in clips, and watch any videos in which you've been tagged.

POKE

To watch videos on Facebook, you'll need the latest Flash Player (available at www.adobe.com/products/flashplayer).

Watching a Video Clip

Whenever one of your friends posts a video, it appears in your News Feed, including a thumbnail of the video along with a play button. Click the **Play** button or anywhere on the thumbnail to run the video. Facebook enlarges the viewer and starts playing the clip.

Play button

*Click **Play**.*

To check out whether one of your Facebook friends has recorded and uploaded any video, check out your friend's Video page by following these steps:

1. Head to your Profile page and in the left menu click **Friends**.

2. Click the name of the friend whose videos you want to view. This takes you to the person's Home page.

3. Click the **Photos** tab.

4. Just above your friend's photos, click the **Videos** link.

5. Click the video you want to watch. Facebook displays the video on its own page.

6. Click the video to start playing it.

To see recent video clips your friends have posted or have been tagged in all in one central location, head to your Video page. To get there from your Home page, click **Photos** (in the left menu) and then click **Video**.

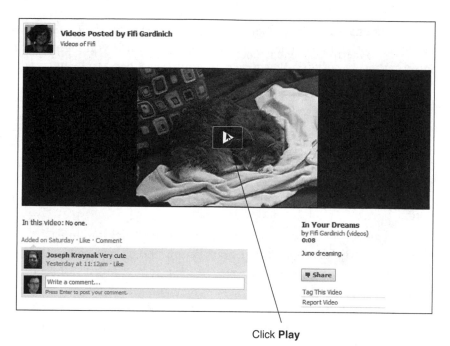

Click **Play**

Watch a friend's video.

Commenting on a Video Clip

Wherever you happen to find a friend's video, you're likely to find a **Write a comment ...** box. Click inside the box, type your comment, and press **Enter**.

You can always delete one of your own comments by clicking **X** (Remove) next to your comment.

WHOA!

If you don't see a Write a comment ... box, someone other than one of your Facebook friends posted the clip or the Facebook member who posted the clip has a privacy setting that prohibits you from commenting on the clip.

Tagging a Video Clip

If a video includes cameo appearances of you or your friends, consider tagging the video to let people know who's in it. When you tag a video, the name of the person you tagged appears below it, and Facebook notifies your friend that he's been tagged. If you tag yourself, that recent activity may appear in your News Feed to keep your friends posted.

> **WHOA!**
>
> As soon as you click the name of a Facebook friend to tag, the tag is applied to the video, and you can't remove it. Only the owner of the video and the person you tagged are authorized to remove the tag. So be sure the person you're tagging wants to be tagged!

To tag a video, first display it on its own page (by clicking on it). Click **Tag This Video**, and then start typing the name of a Facebook friend who appears in the video. As you type, the list of friend names narrows to match what you've typed so far, and you can click a name in the list. To enter another name, press **Enter** or **Return** and then enter the next name. When you're done, click **Done Tagging**.

Watching Videos in Which You've Been Tagged

Turnabout is fair play. Just as you can tag your Facebook friends in videos, they can tag you. If you happen to get tagged, Facebook sends you a notification so you can check out the video. To view all the videos in which you've been tagged, take the following steps:

1. Click **Profile** icon (in the top menu bar). Facebook displays your Profile.

2. Click **Photos** (left menu). Your Photos page appears.

3. Under Photos and Videos of You, click the video you want to watch. The video appears on its own page. (If your Photos page has no Photos and Videos of You section, you haven't been tagged in any photos or videos.)

4. Click the video to play it.

You can de-tag yourself by displaying the video on its own page and then clicking **Remove Tag**.

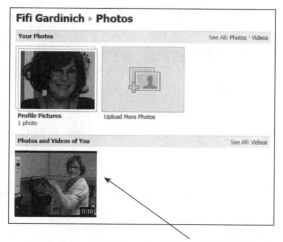

Videos in which you've been tagged

You can view all videos in which you've been tagged.

Recording and Uploading Video Footage

With a digital camcorder or a webcam, you have all the equipment you need to shoot your own video footage. With Facebook's assistance, you can then upload your video to the web and share it with your friends.

In the following sections, we briefly explain Facebook's video guidelines and then show you how to access your Video page, upload video clips stored on your computer, record videos with a webcam, and edit some of the details related to your clip.

Taking Note of Facebook's Video Guidelines

Facebook isn't YouTube. You can't just upload any video footage you think is cool. To keep the spotlight focused on friends, Facebook stipulates that any video clips you choose to upload meet the following conditions.

- Compliant with the Facebook Code of Conduct and Terms of Use. The term of use Facebook probably had in mind here is this one: "You will not post content that is hateful, threatening, pornographic, or that contains nudity or graphic or gratuitous violence."

- Personal in nature. Videos must be of you or your friends, taken by you or your friends, or original art or animation created by you or your friends.

- Does not infringe upon or violate the copyright, trademark, publicity, privacy, or other rights of any third party.

- Does not attempt to circumvent any filtering techniques or technologies Facebook may use to screen content.

WHOA!

If you post video that doesn't adhere to every single one of these guidelines, Facebook may remove the content and perhaps even terminate your account.

Accessing the Video Page

Facebook features everything you need to upload and share video, and all the tools are accessible via the Create a New Video page. To get to there from your Home page, click **Photos** (in the left menu), and then click the **+ Upload Video** button above the photos. The Create a New Video page appears.

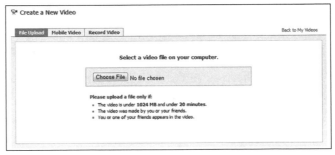

You can record and upload video via the Create a New Video page.

Uploading a Video Clip from Your Computer

If you have any digital video clips lying around on your computer, you can upload them to Facebook. The only limitation (besides Facebook's Code of Conduct) is that the video can be no longer than 20 minutes and no larger than 1024MB (1 gigabyte).

Facebook supports numerous digital video formats, including Mobile Video (*.3g2, *.3gp, *.3gpp), DIVX Video (*.divx), DV Video (*.dv), Windows Media Video (*.asf and *.wmv), AVI Video (*.avi), Flash Video (*.flv, *flv4), MPEG Video (*.mpeg, *.mpe, *.mpg, *.dat), MPEG-4 Video (*.m4v, *.mp4, *.mpeg4), Matroska Format (*.mkv), MOD Video (*.mod), QuickTime Movie (*.mov, *.qt), Nullsoft Video (*.nsv), Ogg Format (*.ogm, *.ogv), TOD (*.tod), M2TS Video (*.m2ts), AVCHD (*.mts), MPEG Transport Stream (*.ts), and DVD Video (*.vob).

To upload a digital video file from your computer, take the following steps:

1. Head to your Home page and click the **Photo** tab.

2. Click **+ Upload Video** (upper right). The Create a New Video page appears.

3. Click **Browse**. The Choose File to Upload dialog box appears.

4. Navigate to the folder where the digital video file is stored, select the file, and click **Open**. Facebook starts uploading it and displays a form you can fill out while you're waiting.

5. Enter any information you want to include with the video, including a title, description, a list of people in the video, and privacy settings to determine who can and can't view the video.

6. Click **Save Info**.

For instructions on how to upload videos from your cell phone or other mobile device, see Chapter 15.

Recording Video Using Your Webcam

If you're in the mood to make and post a spur-of-the-moment video, plug a webcam into your computer, and you instantly convert it into a digital video recorder. With the addition of Facebook, you can now film yourself on the fly and instantly upload the clip to Facebook. Here's what you do:

1. Head to your Profile and click the **Photos** tab.

2. Click **+ Upload Video** (upper right). The Create a New Video page appears.

3. Click the **Record Video** tab. The Adobe Flash Player Settings dialog box appears, asking permission to access your camera and microphone.

4. Click **Allow** and then **Close**. A window appears, showing what your webcam sees right now.

5. Click the **Record** button (the red button with the white dot, last we checked), and then proceed to ham it up in front of the camera. (After you click the record button, it changes into a Stop button.)

6. When you're done with the show, click the **Stop** button.

7. Click **Play** to view the video.

8. Take one of the following steps:

   • If you don't like the clip, click **Reset** and head back to step 5 for a reshoot.

   • If you like the clip, click **Save**. This takes you to the Edit Video page, where you can enter information about the video.

9. Enter any information you want to include with the video, including a title, description, and privacy settings to determine who can and can't view the video. You can also choose a frame of the video to serve as the thumbnail that represents it.

10. Click **Save**. Facebook saves your video and posts it to your Wall and News Feed to share with friends.

FRIEND-LY ADVICE

When recording, try to look at the camera rather than the screen. Otherwise, you appear to be looking away from your audience.

Film yourself live!

Editing Video Information

After you upload or record a video, you can edit any information you entered and make other changes, such as rotating the clip 90 degrees clockwise or counterclockwise (if you shot it at an angle).

To edit the video, click **Profile** (in the top menu), click your **Photos** tab, click **Video** (above your photos), and then click the video you want to edit. This displays the video on its own page, where you can select any of the following options:

- **Share:** Post the video to your Wall and News Feed, or send it as a message attachment to your Facebook friends.
- **Rotate Left:** Rotate the video counterclockwise 90 degrees.
- **Rotate Right:** Rotate the video clockwise 90 degrees.
- **Tag This Video:** Tag yourself or a friend in the video.

- **Edit This Video:** Modify the title, description, or privacy settings associated with the video. You can also tag yourself or your friends in the video and choose a different frame to use as the video's thumbnail.

- **Delete Video:** Remove the video from your Facebook account, which removes it from your Wall and News Feed, too.

- **Embed This Video:** Obtain a code you can add to web pages or blog posts that displays a box in which the video plays. The following section provides additional details about embedding a video.

Embedding a Video

If you have your own website or blog, you can embed your Facebook videos on your web pages or include them in your blog posts. Here's what you do:

1. Click **Profile** (in the top menu), click **Photos** (left menu), click **Video** (above your photos), and click the video you want to embed. The video appears on a page of its own.

2. Click **Embed this Video**. The Embed Your Video box appears.

3. Click in the **Embed code** text box to highlight the code and then press **Ctrl+C** (on a PC) or **Command+C** (on a Mac), to copy it.

4. Open the web page or blog post in which you want to embed the video in HTML view. Web authoring and blogging software typically enable you to edit content in HTML mode (where you can see the tags) or in Visual mode (where the page looks like it will appear to users). In WordPress, for example, you click the **HTML** tab to edit in HTML mode. If you paste the <embed> code in Visual mode, people see the code instead of the video.

5. Click where you want to embed the video.

6. Press **Ctrl+V** (on a PC) or **Command+V** (on a Mac) to insert the embed code.

7. Save your web page or blog post.

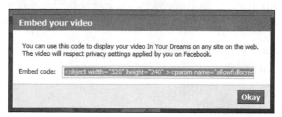

You can embed a Facebook video on a web page or blog post.

Whenever someone views your web page or blog post, a small box appears with a Play button inside it that the visitor can click to play the video. The cool thing is that, because the video is stored on Facebook and not on your web-hosting service, none of your resources are required to play the video—in other words, you're not using up any of your storage space or bandwidth.

Sending a Video Message via E-Mail

Tired of sending plain text messages? Add some spark with a video clip. On Facebook, it's easy—especially if you already uploaded or recorded a clip. To send a video that's already on Facebook (your own video or a Facebook friend's), here's what you do:

1. Display the video on its own page. For example, head to your Profile, click your **Photos** tab, click **Video**, and then click one of your videos; or you can click a video in your News Feed and then click its title (below the video).

2. Click **Share** (to the right of the video). The Post to Profile box opens.

3. Click **Send as a Message Instead**. The Send as a Message box appears.

4. Click in the **To** box and type the name(s) of one or more Facebook friends.

5. Click in the **Message** box and type a message to accompany the video. It's always a good idea to let people know why they might like to watch it.

6. Click **Send Message**.

You can send a video clip as a message attachment to your Facebook friends.

The Least You Need to Know

- To access your videos, click **Profile**, click your **Photos** tab, and click **Video** (above your photos).

- To access your friends' videos, from your Home page, click **Photos** (in the left menu) and then **Video**.

- Videos on Facebook can't contain content that is hateful, threatening, or pornographic, or that contains nudity or graphic or gratuitous violence. In addition, any video you post must be shot by you or a Facebook friend and contain you or at least one of your Facebook friends.

- In the upper right of your Video page is a button for uploading video.

- To comment on a video, click in the **Write a comment ...** box, type your comment, and press **Enter**.

- The Share option next to a video enables you to post the video to your News Feed or send it as a message attachment to your friends.

Getting Organized with Groups

In This Chapter

- Exploring group dynamics on Facebook
- Joining and leaving groups
- Sharing photos, videos, and other cool stuff
- Creating your own group and gathering members
- Engaging in group chats and collaborative writing

You and your friends on Facebook form a tightly knit clique, but Facebook also allows you to wander off and mingle more intimately with friends and others in *groups*. Groups are useful for gathering former classmates; sharing information among family members; meeting people who share similar goals, values, or interests; facilitating communication among members of an organization; and so on. And you don't even have to be Facebook friends to do it.

In this chapter, we show you how to join a group, form your own groups, engage in discussions, and share stuff with your fellow group members.

Understanding Groups: Open, Closed, and Secret

Facebook Groups are like gatherings around the water cooler, where you can wander away from your News Feed and Wall to enter discussions and share with friends and nonfriends alike in a more theme-oriented environment. On Facebook, you can create or join the following three types of groups:

- **Open:** Open groups allow Facebook members—friends and nonfriends alike—to share common interests and passions. They're great for promoting a political candidate, organizing a movement, or even networking with people in a particular field.

- **Closed:** Exclusive areas where only selected Facebook friends hang out. For example, you can create a group for the South Vernon High School class of 1998 and allow only members of that class to join.

- **Secret:** Super-secret, invitation-only clubs that don't even show up in Facebook search results. Secret groups are great for when you don't want outsiders on Facebook knowing what you're up to.

FRIEND-LY ADVICE

If you're working on a project with others, you can create a secret work group where members can discuss ideas, collaborate on solving problems, monitor progress, and schedule meetings.

Exploring Existing Groups

The first encounter most Facebook members have with Groups is when they receive an invitation from a friend to join a group. (More information about responding to such invitations is provided later in this chapter.) However, you don't need to wait for an invitation to get involved in group activities. You can be more proactive by browsing groups or searching for groups that interest you.

Searching for a Group

If you'd like to check out groups that focus on a specific interest or topic, search for groups by keyword or phrase. Here's how:

1. Click in the **Search** box (in the top menu), type a keyword or two or three, and then click the **Search** button (the one with the magnifying glass on it) or press **Enter.** Facebook displays the top items that match your search entry. The search results may include people, groups, Pages, posts by friends, and other items.

2. Click **Groups** (in the left menu).

3. Scroll down the list to browse available groups that match your search criteria.

4. When you reach the bottom of the list, you can click **See More Results** to view the next 10 groups in the list.

Search for an interest

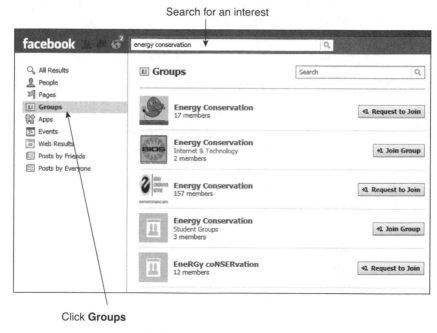

Click **Groups**

Find a group that interests you.

Finding Groups Through Your Friends

Chances are good that if one of your close Facebook friends joins a group, it's worth checking out. Friends can turn you on to groups in the following ways.

- **Invitation:** A friend can send you an invitation to join the group. Accept the invitation, and you're in.

- **Your News Feed:** Whenever a friend joins a group, that activity may show up in your News Feed with a link to the group, unless your friend chose to remove that item from his Recent Activity area after joining the group. Click the link to head to the group's Home page.

- **Friends' Walls:** Whenever someone joins a group, the activity is posted on the person's Wall under Recent Activities. By pulling up a friend's Profile and checking her Wall, you can check out which groups your friend has recently joined.

To find out how to prevent the Groups app from posting updates to your News Feed or hide the fact that you joined a particular group, skip ahead to the section "Joining a Group."

Checking Out a Group

After you've found a few groups that possibly match your interests, you can inspect them more closely. Click the group's name or the picture that represents it, and the group's Home page pops up.

An open group's Home page lets you sample the group before joining it.

A closed group's Home page severely restricts access for nonmembers. You may see some basic information, but you probably won't see the Wall, Discussion Board, or member list until you join.

Getting Involved in a Group

To get involved in a group and share with its members, you must first join the group. As you'll see in the following sections, joining and leaving a group are two of the easiest things you can do on Facebook.

Joining a Group

All you need to do to join an open group on Facebook is click **Join Group** next to the group you want to join and then click the **Join** button when prompted to confirm, and you gain instant access. To join a closed group, click **Request to Join** next to the group you want to join. You then have to wait for the administrator to confirm your request. You don't have to keep checking; when you're allowed in, you receive a notification letting you know. If your request is denied or ignored, you don't receive notification.

Leaving a Group

If you happen to lose interest in a group, you can leave at any time. Click the **Groups** icon (in the left menu). Click the name or photo of the group you want to leave, click **Leave Group** (last option below the member list on the right), and click **Remove** when prompted to confirm. That's it. You're outta there. If you're the only member of the group and you leave, the group disappears.

Conversing in Groups

Posting content to a group is no different than posting content to your Wall or News Feed. When you're ready to post a message to the group, click in the **Write something ...** box, type your message, and click **Share**.

Share with the group via the group Wall.

In addition to posting status updates, you can post a link, photo, or video clip, just as you can on your Wall or News Feed. Just click one of the following icons in the Publisher:

- **Link:** To post a link to another website or page, click **Link** and then type or paste the site or page address in the resulting text box and click **Attach**.

- **Photo:** To share a photo or take a photo with your webcam and share it with the group, click **Photo** and then click either **Upload a Photo** or **Take a Photo** and follow the on-screen instructions. See Chapter 7 for more about sharing photos on Facebook.

- **Video:** To share a video clip with the group, click **Video**, and then click **Record a Video** or **Upload a Video** and follow the on-screen instructions.

You can attach a link, photo, or video clip to your status update before or after composing your text entry, or you can omit the text entry and post the item without adding any commentary.

Unsubscribing from a Conversation

As a member of a group you receive a notification whenever some-one comments on something you posted. If these notifications get annoying, you can unsubscribe from the conversation. Just go to the group, find the conversation, and click its **Unsubscribe** link. The Unsubscribe link turns into the Subscribe link, which you can click if you change your mind.

Creating Your Own Group

If you think all the existing groups on Facebook are lame-o, create your own group. It's easy; follow these steps:

1. From your Home page, click **Create Group ...** (in the left menu). The Create Group dialog box appears.

2. Type a name for the group.

3. Click in the **Members** box, start typing the name of a friend to add to the group, and when you see the name you want, click it. Continue to type and click to add more names.

4. Click the button next to Privacy, and choose the type of group you want to create: Open, Closed, or Secret.

5. Click **Create**. Facebook creates the group.

When you're done creating the group, head to the group's Home page, click **Add a profile picture**, and then upload a photo or snap a photo using your webcam. It's always nice to have a photo for your group.

From the group's Home page, you can change the group's settings by clicking **Edit Group** (in the right column). To change informa-tion you entered about the group, click **Basic Information** and edit the information as desired. You can change the group name, its pri-vacy setting, and whether only administrators can approve requests to join; set up group e-mail; or add a description of the group, which is always a good idea.

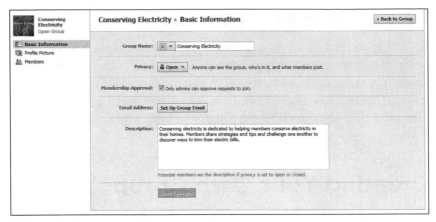

Edit your group settings.

Creating a Group E-Mail Address

A group e-mail address enables anyone in the group to send an e-mail message to the address so Facebook distributes it to all group members. The e-mail address will be something@groups.facebook. com, and you'll supply the "something." You can't change it, so think of something good.

To create a group e-mail address, go to your Home page and click the name of the group (in the left menu). Click **Edit Group** (right column), and then click the **Set Up Group Email** button. Type the beginning of the e-mail address (no spaces), such as group-name@ groups.facebook.com, and then click **Create Email**.

Create a group e-mail address.

Adding Friends to the Group

Although you probably added friends to the group when you first created it, you can add more friends at any time. Head to the group's page by clicking its name in the left menu on your Home page. Then, click **Add Friends to Group** in the column on the right. The Add Friends to Group dialog box appears. Start typing the name of a friend, and when you see the name you want, click it. Continue to type and click to add more names. When you're ready to add the specified friends, click the **Add** button.

Making Someone Else an Administrator

When you create a group, you become its administrator. Only you have the power to edit the group and add people to and remove them from the group. If you'd like to share your administrator duties, you can make other group members administrators. Here's how:

1. On your Home page, click the name of the group (left menu).

2. At the top of the Members list (right column), click **See All**. Facebook displays all of the group's members.

3. Click **Make Admin** next to the name/photo of the person to whom you want to grant administrator privileges.

> **POKE**
>
> Just above the Members list is a **View Admins** link you can click to view only group members who have administrator status. Next to each administrator's name/photo is a Remove Admin link you can click to revoke the person's privileges, if necessary. Only administrators can view and remove administrators.

Removing Group Members

To kick someone out of the group, first pull up the member list. From your Home page, on the left menu, click the name of the group in which the person is a member. Above the Members list (on the right), click **See All**. Click the **X** next to the name/photo of the member you want to eject. The Remove box appears prompting you to confirm the removal. To ban the member permanently from the group, click **Ban Permanently**. When you're ready to do the deed, click **Confirm**.

To kick an administrator out of the group, you need to remove the person's administrator status first, as explained in the previous section.

Sharing Photos Within the Group

You can share photos within a group that only those who belong to the group have access to. This is great if you create a group for your family or your graduating class and want to share photos privately.

To view or add photos, head to your Home page and click the group's name (in the left menu). In the right column, click **View Photos**. From this page, you can check out any photo albums that group members have created or create your own albums. For more about photo sharing, see Chapter 7.

Creating an Event

If you're planning a special event for the group, such as a monthly meeting or a holiday party, consider using the Facebook Event feature to invite everyone and keep track of who's planning to show up.

To announce an event, head to the group's page and click **Create Event** (in the right column). The Create an Event form appears. Enter the requested information, including the date and time, what you're planning, and where. By default, Facebook will invite all members of the group. If you want to be more selective, remove the checkmark next to Invite Members of the Host Group, and then click the **Select Guests** button to invite your friends individually. You may also want to remove the checkmark next to **Anyone can view and RSVP (public) event**, so you don't end up with thousands of unintended guests, which could culminate in the ultimate of surprise parties. You also have the option to **Show the guest list on the event page** and **Add Event Photo**. When you're done entering your preferences, click **Create Event**.

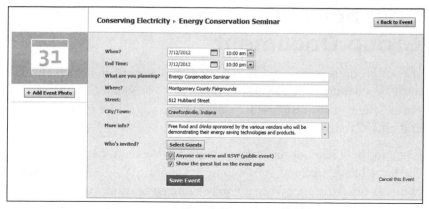

Create an event.

To edit the event, head to your Home page, click **Events** (in the left menu), click the event you want to edit, and click the **Edit Event** button.

For more about Facebook's Event feature, check out Chapter 11.

Chatting with the Group

Few things in life are more invigorating than chatting with a group, and now Facebook has made that possible. With Group Chat, everyone in the group can join the discussion as if you're all sitting in the same room. Nobody outside the group can "listen in" or intrude. To start chatting, head to the group's page and click **Chat with Group** (right column). (If you don't see the Chat with Group link, click **Go Online to Chat** first.) A small chat window pops up from the bottom of the screen. Type something to get the conversation rolling and press **Enter**. Assuming other group members are online, logged in to Facebook, and available to chat, a chat window appears on their screens, too, and they can join in the conversation.

For more about Facebook Chat, see Chapter 10.

Collaborating on a Group Document

If your group is primarily work-related, you might need to collaborate on documents, and you can do so in a Facebook Group. To create a new document to start working on, access the group's page and click **Create a Doc** (right column).

Click in the **Title** box and type a name for the document. Click in the large blank area and start typing your draft. You can also paste contents into this area. When you're done composing your draft, click the **Create Doc** button. A preview of the document appears in each group member's News Feed along with a link they can click to view the full document. As they view the document, they can click the **Edit** icon to enter their own changes.

Type a title   Click **Create Doc**

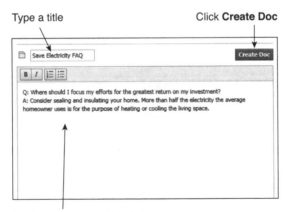

Start composing your document

Create a document to collaborate on with group members.

POKE

When the group has one or more documents, the column on the right of the group's page contains a Docs section with links to recently created or edited documents.

The Least You Need to Know

- Groups enable you to mingle with Facebook friends and others and engage in discussions outside the more public venues of Walls and News Feeds.

- To find groups that might interest you, click in the **Search** box (top menu), type a descriptive word or two for the type of group you want, press **Enter**, and then click **Groups** (left menu).

- To create a group, click **Home** (top menu), **Create Group ...** (left menu), and follow the on-screen cues.

- To join a group, click the **Join Group** or **Request to Join** button next to the group's name.

- On your Home page, the left menu contains links to all of the groups you belong to.

- After accessing a group's page, check the right column for a list of group members and for links to chat with the group, add friends, create a document or event, and leave the group.

Chatting with Friends in Real Time

In This Chapter

- Chatting with friends using Facebook's instant-messaging tool
- Starting and ending a Chat session
- Engaging in audio/video and group chats
- Hiding from friends when you don't want to be bothered
- Customizing Chat

When friends are online, you may have the opportunity to carry on a conversation with them using Facebook's Chat application. If you're familiar with AIM, Yahoo! Messenger, or any of the many other instant-messaging programs out there, you know the drill: you select the person you want to chat with from your list of friends, click the **Chat** button, and start typing. As you chat, whatever you type appears on her screen, and whatever she types appears on yours. (If you're not familiar with instant messaging, don't worry—it's easier than e-mail, and we take you through the process step by step.) Facebook Chat includes a couple extra bells and whistles, including group chat and audio/video calling via Facebook + Skype.

In this chapter, you discover how to initiate and navigate a typical Facebook Chat session, set your chat options, and use friend lists to more effectively track the people you're chatting with.

Let's Chat!

Compared to other chat programs, Facebook Chat is the stripped-down, no-frills model. Assuming one of your friends is logged in and online (more about the online thing in a minute), initiating a Chat session is a breeze. Here's what you do:

1. Click the thumbnail of the friend you want to chat with (left column, bottom). Or click **Chat** (lower-right corner of any Facebook Page) and click the name of the friend you want to chat with. Either way, a chat box appears. (Facebook displays a sidebar that lists the friends you message and chat with most often, so you can easily spot them.)

2. Type a message and press **Enter**. Your message pops up in the chat box on your screen and your friend's screen. Assuming your friend responds, his message pops up right below yours.

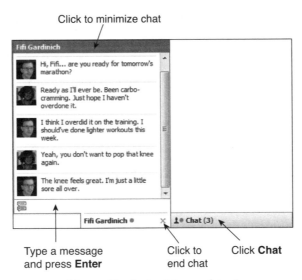

Chat on Facebook with your friends.

You can carry on Chat sessions with more than one friend at a time. Each Chat session appears in its own box with its own tab. To change from one Chat session to another, click the tab for the friend you want to chat with.

You can click the bar at the top of any chat window to make the window disappear without closing it. A tab for the window appears (typically the bottom right of the screen), and a red balloon icon appears to notify you whenever someone sends you a chat message. If your speakers are on and the volume's turned up, you'll also hear an audio cue whenever someone sends you a new message.

When you're ready to end a session and close the chat window, just click the **X** next to your friend's name.

If one of your friends sends you a message to start a Chat session, a chat box pops up, allowing you to reply.

That's it. Short chapter, huh? Well, not exactly. Chat includes some additional features, and we spend the rest of the chapter exploring those.

> **POKE**
>
> On Facebook, you can chat only with friends, not strangers. To contact someone who's not your friend, head to the person's Profile and click the link to send them a message. For more about sending messages, see Chapter 6. For details on friending someone, see Chapter 4.

Viewing and Deleting Your Chat History

Facebook keeps a log of your chat history so you can pick up where you left off when you ended your last Chat session with a friend. When you begin a new Chat session, you can see the last few lines of your previous session.

You can clear the chat history at any time to prevent snoopy family members or officemates from nosing in on your business or just reduce the clutter of messages. Scroll to the top of the chat window and click **Clear Window**.

Facebook also stores your chats as messages, so you have an entire history of your correspondence with everyone via messages, chat, text messaging, and e-mail. To view your messages, head to your Home page and click **Messages** (in the left menu). For more about Facebook's Messages, see Chapter 6.

Click **Clear Window**

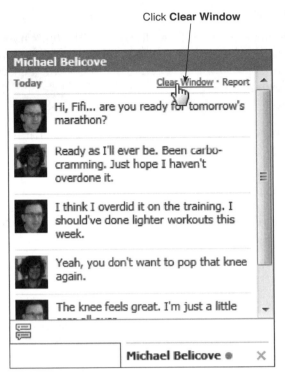

The chat history lets you and your friend pick up where you left off.

Going Offline or Back Online

Unless you tell Facebook otherwise, whenever you're logged in, you're online and ready to chat. If a friend opens his Chat menu, your name appears on that menu, and he can click it to start chatting with you. If you choose to go offline, you're invisible and friends can't tell you're online and can't bug you. To go offline or come back online, here's what you do:

- **Go offline:** Click **Chat > Options > Go Offline**.

- **Go online:** Click **Chat**.

You can make yourself available to specific friends or friend lists exclusively (and hide from others). More information on these options can be found near the end of this chapter.

> **POKE**
>
> When you're offline, a gray dot appears next to Chat in your Chat bar, your status is shown as (Offline), and your name doesn't appear on your friends' Chat menus. When you or your friends are online and are chatting, a solid green dot appears next to your name. When you or a friend is online but inactive (haven't done anything on Facebook for at least 10 minutes), a green quarter-moon icon appears next to the name.

To hide, click **Chat >
Option > Go Offline**

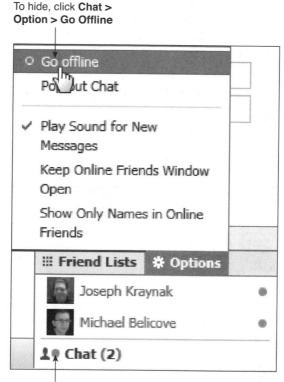

To go online to chat, click **Chat**

You can go offline to be incommunicado.

Engaging in a Video Call

Facebook has teamed up with Skype to offer video calls, so you can hear and see the person you're talking to, assuming you and your friend both have webcams connected to your computers. If either of you doesn't have a webcam, but your computers are equipped with a sound card, speakers, and a microphone, you can still call one another without the video component.

To start a video call, do one of the following:

- Head to your friend's Profile page and click the **Call** button near the top of your friend's profile.

- Click **Chat** (lower-right corner of any Facebook page) and click the name of the friend you want to chat with. The chat box appears. Click the **Start a video call** button in the upper right (it looks like a video camera).

If this is your first time using the video call feature, Facebook prompts you to install the Facebook Video Calling Plugin. Follow the on-screen instructions to complete the installation.

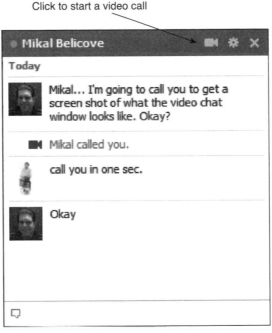

Click to start a video call

Engage in video calls with your friends.

WHOA!

As we were writing this book, Facebook was in the process of rolling out the video call feature to selected users. If you don't see the Call or Start a video call button, ask a friend who has the feature to try calling you. When your friend calls you, a dialog box appears on your screen prompting you to install the Facebook Video Calling Plugin. Follow the on-screen instructions to complete the installation.

After you install the Facebook Video Calling Plugin, Facebook places the call. A dialog box appears on your friend's screen asking if she wants to accept the call. Assuming she accepts, you can start talking. You should see a window that streams live video of your friend, and your friend should see a window that streams live video of you.

Start talking.

If your friend is online but unavailable, Facebook prompts you to leave a recorded message. Click **Record Message** and follow the on-screen cues to record and send your message.

Chatting in a Group

Whether you're planning an outing or just hanging out, looping other friends into your conversation comes in very handy, and it's easy with Facebook. To chat with a group of friends who are all online, start a chat with one friend as you normally do, and then click the **Add Friends to Chat** button in the upper-right corner of the chat window and choose the friend you want to add.

Click **Add Friends to Chat**

Chat in a group.

WHOA!

According to Facebook, Video Calling is for individual Facebook members to enable friend-to-friend communication only. As we were writing this edition of the book, Video Calling is not available for Facebook Pages. (For more about Facebook Pages, see Chapter 17.)

Setting Your Chat Options

Although Facebook Chat is slim and trim, it does offer a few optional features, including a larger chat window and audio cues. In the following sections, we show you how to access these accessories.

Pop-Out Chat

Those teeny-tiny chat boxes are nice for exchanging a few short pleasantries with your Facebook friends, but if you're engaged in a deep conversation or are chatting with multiple friends, they can be very difficult to manage. Fortunately, Facebook enables you to trade in those chat boxes for a full-size chat window devoted solely to talking amongst your friends.

To display the chat window, click **Chat > Options > Pop out Chat**. The chat window appears. To change from one Chat session to another, click the name of the friend you want to chat with.

You can close the window by clicking the **X** in the upper-right corner. This doesn't end your Chat session; it just returns you to the pop-in chat box that appears at the bottom of the Facebook screen. You can also return to the pop-in chat box by clicking **Options > Pop in Chat**.

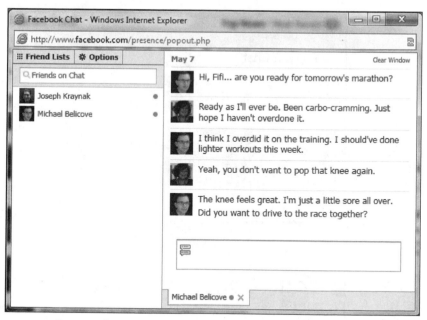

Pop-out chat gives you a dedicated window in which to converse.

Play Sound for New Messages

Assuming you have speakers or earphones plugged into your computer and they're turned on, whenever someone sends you a message, Facebook dings you. Actually, it sounds more like the popping noise you make when you smack your lips. You can toggle this option on or off; click **Chat > Options > Play Sound for New Messages**.

Keep Online Friends Window Open

When you click **Chat**, the menu that pops up is called the Online Friends Window. If you click to do something else on Facebook, like head back to your Home page, the window disappears. If you'd like the Online Friends Window to remain open as you cruise around Facebook, click **Chat > Options > Keep Online Friends Window Open**.

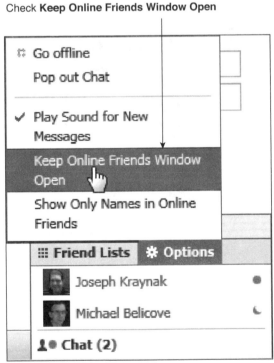

You can keep the Online Friends Window open while you wander Facebook.

Show Only Names in Online Friends

Unless you specify otherwise, Facebook displays the names and Profile photos of your friends in the Online Friends Window. You can omit the photos to make room for displaying more names. Click **Chat > Options > Show Only Names in Online Friends**.

Setting Friend List Options

With the Friend Lists feature, described in Chapter 4, you can keep lists of friends separate. This can come in very handy when you're chatting online. You can display friends by lists, go offline with one list while remaining online with another, or even choose to engage in an intimate discussion with your BFF without the distractions from other friends who may want to strike up a conversation.

Display or Hide a Friend List

When numerous friends are online chatting, the Online Friends Window can get awfully cluttered. One way to reduce the clutter and more effectively manage Chat sessions is to group your friends by friend list.

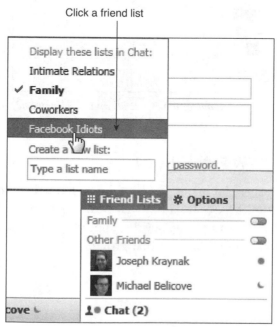

You can group online chatters by friend list.

To turn a friend list on or off, click **Chat > Friend Lists**, and click the list you want to display or hide. A checkmark indicates the friend list is displayed.

Go Offline or Online with a Group of Friends

When you group chatters by friend lists, you can go offline with one or more groups of friends while remaining online with others. Rest the mouse pointer on the icon to the right of the friend list you want to be offline with and, when you see **Go Offline**, click the icon.

Click to go offline with one group of friends

You can go offline with one group of friends and remain online with others.

Create a New Friend List

You can create a friend list on the fly. Click **Chat > Friend Lists**, and then click in the **Create a new list** box. Type a name for the new list, and press **Enter**. The new list appears, and Facebook automatically places you online with that group.

Drag friends to the new friend list, click **Chat** (lower-right corner of the screen), mouse over the name of the friend list you want to add friends to, and click the **edit** link. The Edit List box appears. Click the picture/name of each friend you want to include in the list. Selected friends appear with a dark blue background and a checkmark over their pictures. (You can click a selected friend to remove the person from the group.) After selecting all the friends you want in this group, click the **Save List** button.

Select friends to include

Click **Save List**

You can create a new friend list on the fly.

POKE

Facebook Chat is supported by a number of non-Facebook instant-messaging clients, including iChat, Adium, and Pidgin, all of which enable you to chat with your friends even if you're not logged in to Facebook.

The Least You Need to Know

- To strike up a conversation with a friend who's currently online, click **Chat** (bottom right) and then click the friend's name.
- To go offline and hide from friends who may want to chat with you, click **Chat > Options > Go Offline**.
- To go back online, click **Chat**.
- To display a dedicated chat window, click **Chat > Options > Pop out Chat**.
- To go offline with a certain friend list, click **Chat** and then click the green switch to the right of the friend list. Click the switch again to go back online.

Partay! Tracking and Announcing Events

In This Chapter

- Meeting your own personal events planner
- Finding out what's happening
- Responding to an invitation
- Planning your own event and announcing it

Party at Mikal's house, Saturday night, 6 pm till ?:?? am, BYOB! Food, ice, and entertainment provided! Be sure to RSVP, so we know how much pizza to order!

Yep, announcing an event on Facebook is as easy and inexpensive as that. No mailing invitations. No phone calls, wrong numbers, or answering machines. All you do is compose your event announcement, set your preferences, choose the friends you want to invite, and wait for them to RSVP or just show up. Whether you're planning a small get-together or a major public gathering like a benefit, concert, or grand opening, Facebook's Events app (application) has everything you need to spread the word, take a head count of likely attendees, and keep everyone in the loop regarding any change of plans.

If you're planning an upcoming event, this chapter can play a key role in your event planning. If you're just looking for something to do, you'll discover how to tune in to announcements of upcoming events and respond to any invitations you happen to receive.

Accessing and Navigating the Events App

Whenever you're planning an event or just in the mood for some action, head to the Events app. To get there from your Home page, click **Events** (in the left menu). The Events page appears, supplying you with a list of any events you've been invited to along with a link for creating an event. Consider the Events page your launch pad for doing everything else explained in this chapter.

Click **Events**   Check current events

Create an event
and send invitations

Check friends' events
and birthdays

The Events app lets you check upcoming events and plan new events.

Checking Scheduled Events

Why deal with the hassle of planning an event when you can just show up at someone else's shindig, trash his space, eat his food, and head home for a much-needed nap? With Facebook's Events app, you have access to your own party line 24/7. You can check out events your friends have in the works; poke around for events that might grab your attention; or search for specific events by school, location, favorite bands, favorite comedians, or anything else that twists your imagination. The following sections show you how.

Poking Around for Events

The quickest way to keep tabs on upcoming events, friends' events, past events, and birthdays is to use the options that appear below Events after you click it. Click **Friends' Events**, for example, and you can check out all the events your Facebook friends are planning to attend or are hosting.

Click to get more information

Check out your friends' events.

Click the event's title to find out more about it, including more about the date, time, and location; a full description of the event; a list of confirmed guests as well as people who've said they're not coming or may be coming and people who haven't yet responded to their invitations; any comments guests have chosen to post on the event's Wall; and links you can use to contact the person who created the event or who invited you to attend.

FRIEND-LY ADVICE

Scroll to the bottom of the event and click **Export** to download it as a calendar event or send it as an e-mail to the e-mail address you have on file with Facebook. If you download it as a calendar event and you have a scheduling program on your computer, such as Microsoft Outlook, that program may automatically import the event. Otherwise, you're prompted to save the event as an ".ical" file, which you can then import into your scheduling program, such as Apple iCal, Microsoft Outlook, or Google Calendar.

You can let the hosts know whether you're attending, may be attending, or will not be attending the event by clicking the appropriate button in the upper-right corner of the event's page. (More details about RSVP-ing are provided later in this chapter.)

If the event planner allows it, you can click the **+ Select Guests to Invite** button (left column last we checked) to invite your friends. If the event planner chose not to allow guests to invite friends, the button doesn't appear.

When you click an event, you get the full scoop.

Searching and Browsing Events

Bored? Nothing to do on a Friday night? Wrong! There's plenty going on. You just don't know about it. Now with Facebook, you can search for and browse events near or far to find potentially engaging activities.

Perhaps the best way to search for an event is to head to your Home page, click **Events**, and then use the Events page to check out what all your friends are doing.

To expand your horizons beyond what your Facebook friends are up to, you can search for events by type of event, the name of a band or comedian, a school name, location (city or town), special interest (like volleyball), and so on. Here's what you do to search for events:

1. Click in the **Search** box (top menu), type one or two words describing the sort of event you're interested in (for example, "slam poetry chicago"), and press **Enter**. Facebook displays Events, Groups, Pages, and other stuff that matches your search instructions.

2. Click **Events** (in the left menu). Facebook narrows the list to show only events.

Perform a search

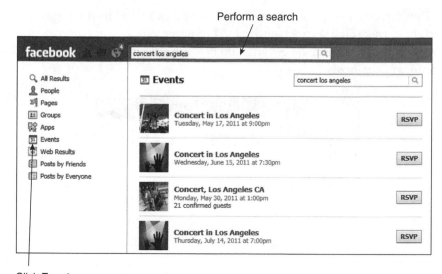

Click **Events**

Perform a broad search and then narrow the results to events only.

RSVP-ing an Event You Plan to Attend

If you've been invited to an event or plan on attending an event open to the public, RSVP the hosts to let them know whether you're coming, not coming, or unsure. Besides being the polite thing to do, your RSVP serves several practical purposes. For one, it helps the hosts take a head count, so they can prepare for the hungry, thirsty hordes that are likely to show up.

Perhaps more importantly, your RSVP (especially if you're planning to attend) spreads the word about the event. Your RSVP is status update worthy, and it shows up in your News Feed, on your Wall, and in some cases—if you edit your Event preferences to allow for this—on all your friends' News Feeds. You also show up in the event's Confirmed Guests list and, as everyone knows, a crowd usually draws a crowd.

By RSVP-ing, you get a perk, too. If the hosts change plans or cancel the event and are responsible enough to make those changes on Facebook, you receive a notification on Facebook and via e-mail (assuming you didn't disable e-mail notifications for Events).

RSVP-ing is a snap. Just head to the event's page and in the upper-right corner, click **I'm Attending**, **Maybe**, or **No**. If you received a personal invitation via e-mail, you can use the same options to inform your hosts.

Be polite by RSVP-ing to the hosts.

FRIEND-LY ADVICE

Consider expressing your eager anticipation or whatever else on the event Wall to get others excited about attending the event.

Announcing Your Own Special Event

Whether you're planning a family get-together, a slam poetry competition, or a political rally, you need to get the word out to your people. The easiest way to do this is to create an event on Facebook. All you do is specify the who, what, when, where, and why and then select the friends you want to invite. Facebook does the rest, sending out all your invitations in the blink of an eye. If plans change, just edit the event, and Facebook notifies everyone on your guest list!

In the following sections, we show you how to create and customize an event, invite guests, take a head count, print a guest list, and more. And in the unfortunate circumstance that your event fizzles, we even show you how to cancel it.

FRIEND-LY ADVICE

Be polite. If you're invited to an event, RSVP. Don't invite people you don't really know to a highly personal event like a birthday party or baby shower. And if you're coordinating an event, don't over-promote it or send too many reminders to your friends.

Creating an Event

Creating an event is easy. Start the process using one of the following methods, depending on whether you're planning the event for your Facebook friends or for a Facebook Group you administer:

- **Event for Friends:** From your Home page, click **Events** (in the left menu). Click **+ Create an Event**. The Create an Event page appears, prompting you to enter details about the event.

- **Group Event:** Pull up the group's page, as explained in Chapter 9, and then click **Create an Event** (in the right column). By creating the event from the group's page, you'll have the option to invite all group members simply by clicking a checkbox.

Enter details about the event.

However you choose to initiate the process, the Create an Event screen appears, prompting you to enter details about the event. Specify the event's date and time, add a brief description of the event, enter its location, and use the More info? box to enter additional details. When specifying a location, this is typically a name of a place everyone you're inviting is familiar with. If you're not sure whether everyone is familiar with it, click **Add street address** and type a street address and the name of the city or town.

> **WHOA!**
>
> Think twice about entering contact information in your event description. People can contact you through Facebook. You don't need to risk having your e-mail address or phone number fall into the wrong hands.

When you're done entering details about the event, click **Select Guests**, click the people you want to invite, enter e-mail addresses of anyone you want to invite who's not a Facebook member, and click **Save and Close**. Below the Select Guests button are additional options that vary depending on whether you're creating a group event. You might see the following:

- **Invite members of the host group <group name>:** This option appears only if you're creating a Facebook Group event. It enables you to easily invite all group members.

- **Anyone can view and RSVP (public event):** Unless you want to open this event to everyone on Facebook, uncheck this option. If you uncheck it, another option appears: Guests can invite Friends. You probably want to make sure this option is deselected, too. If you want friends to be able to bring a significant other, you might add that to the More info? box.

- **Show the guest list on the event page:** To keep everyone posted as to who's been invited and plans on attending, make sure this option is checked.

To add a photo for the event, click the **+ Add Event Photo** button, and use the resulting dialog box to upload a photo. We recommend adding a photo if for no other reason than to make the event seem more festive.

When you're done fleshing out your event, click the **Create Event** button. Facebook displays the event's page and sends invitations to all of the invitees.

Carefully inspect your event for any errors. If you see something that's not right, click **Edit Event**, enter your changes, and click **Save Event**. (If you wandered off to do something else on Facebook, you can always pull up your event from your Home page by clicking **Events** in the left menu.)

Click to edit the event

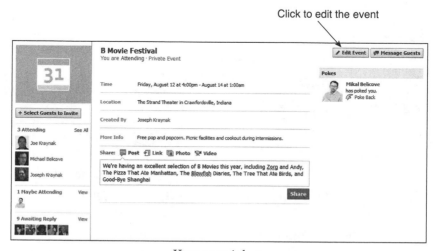

Your event is born.

Keeping Your Guests in the Loop

As the date and time for the event nears, keep your guests excited about it and let them know of any changes in plans. You can do this by posting to the event's Wall or by messaging the guests directly. Use the event's Wall to generate buzz. Send a message to distribute critical information, such as a change in date, time, or venue (location).

To send a message, head to the event's page and click the **Message Guests** button (upper right). By default, Facebook addresses the message to **All**, meaning everyone you invited. To change that, open the Attendees list and select your preference: Attending, Maybe Attending, or Not Yet Replied. Type a subject and message and then click the **Send** button.

Send guests a message

Post to the Wall

Post text, links, photos, or video to the event's Wall.

If you need help planning or managing an event, consider adding an administrator. On the event's page, click **See All** (on the left, just above the list of guests who are attending) and then click **Make Admin** next to the person you want to promote to administrator.

Get some friends to help.

The Least You Need to Know

- To fire up the Events app from your Home page, click the **Events** icon in the left menu.

- After you click **Events**, more options appear enabling you to view friends' events, birthdays, and past events.

- If you're invited to an event, be sure to RSVP. It's the polite thing to do and keeps you in the loop.

- Use the **Search** box in the top menu to search for events, and then click **Events** in the left menu to show only events in the search results.

- To announce your own event, click **Events** (left menu), click the **+ Create an Event** button (upper right), and then follow the on-screen cues.

Taking Notes ... and Sharing Them

12

In This Chapter

- Grasping the basic concept of Facebook Notes
- Reading and commenting on notes—yours, a friend's, a business's, or notes about you
- Posting and sharing notes
- Importing blog entries as notes
- Passing notes in private

After about 60 seconds on Facebook, you know what a status update is, but ask most members what a Facebook Note is, and you'll probably get a blank stare—or the person will fudge and make up some answer like, "A note is more like a reminder to yourself."

Well, that's not quite right. A Facebook Note is much more than that, as you'll see in this chapter.

What Are Notes Exactly?

Notes are Facebook's answer to blogging. If you're not sure what blogging is all about, think of it as journaling or keeping a diary, with two primary differences:

- **Blogging is public (usually).** When you post a blog entry, it appears online where anyone can look at it. Facebook's Notes feature can give you more privacy than a typical blog because, by default, only your Facebook friends are privy to what you post.

- **Blogging is interactive.** People can comment on your blog entries if you let them, and usually you want to let them because, well, that's sorta the point of blogging—you post something and it sparks discussion. Blogging is all about creating an open forum where people can freely exchange information, observations, insights, and opinions. In addition, the more activity your blog entries inspire, the more search engine traffic you attract.

In the world of Facebook, you use notes instead of status updates when you have more to say. In addition, while status updates are exclusively of the plain-text variety, you can format a note using HTML (hypertext markup language) tags, such as <bold> for bold, <i> for italics, and <u> for an underline. In other words, you can get a little fancier with your formatting.

If you already have a blog, don't worry about having to pull double duty. Near the end of this chapter, we show you how to set up an RSS feed on Facebook that automatically pulls entries from your existing blog into Facebook and displays your entries as notes. Pretty cool, eh?

Entering the Notes Zone

Notes is a Facebook app (application). To access the Notes app, head to your Home page and click **Notes** (in the left menu). (You may need to click **More**, below the list of apps, to bring Notes into view.) The Notes page appears displaying recent note activity, if any—friends' notes, your own, and notes about you. This page also provides a button (upper right) for writing a note of your own.

Click **Notes**

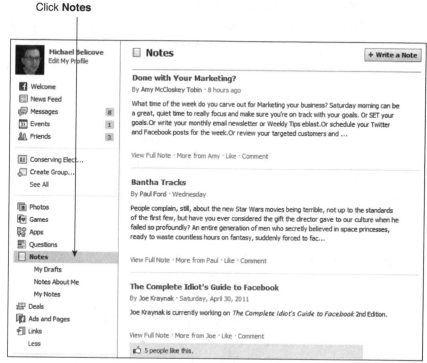

The Notes page, where you can access all your Notes features.

Perusing Your Friends' Notes

The Notes page displays excerpts of notes your Facebook friends have recently posted. You can view a note on a page of its own by clicking the note's title or the **View Full Note** link above the comment box. To view all notes a friend has posted, click your friend's name to head to her Home page and then click **Notes** (left menu). The resulting list displays notes by your friend. To view notes about your friend, click **Notes About**.

When viewing the complete note, you can subscribe to your friend's notes. Under **Subscribe** (to the left of the note), click **<friend's name>'s Notes** and then click the **Subscribe Now** button. This adds an entry to your browser's Feeds menu, giving you quick access to your friends' notes, regardless of whether you're logged on to Facebook.

Commenting on Existing Notes

When your friends post notes, they usually welcome comments. To post a comment, click **Comment** (below the note), type your comment, and press **Enter**. When you do, the friend who wrote the note and anyone else who already left a comment is notified, which sometimes results in even more comments.

Liking a Friend's Note

Whether you're viewing an excerpt or a full note, you can choose to like it, which adds the note to your list of items you like and posts a status update notifying your friends that you like it. This is a quick way of sharing the note with your friends. The next section shows you how to add some commentary to the note while sharing it or send it as a message to a friend.

Sharing a Friend's Note

Do you want to help your friend's note go viral? Then share it. You can share a note by posting it to your News Feed and Wall, where it shows up as a link, or you can share the link by sending a message to your Facebook friends.

To share your friend's note with all your friends via your News Feed and Wall, click the **Share** link, type a brief message explaining why you found the note worthy of sharing, and click **Share**.

To send the note to select friends via a message, click the **Share** link, click **Send as a Message instead**, and then compose and send your message as explained in Chapter 6.

Posting a New Note

To post a note, pull up your Home page, click **Notes** (left menu), and click the **+ Write a Note** button. The Write a Note page appears. Click in the **Title** box and type a brief, descriptive, and compelling title for your note (otherwise, nobody will want to read it). Click in the **Body** box and type whatever you want to say. You can format the text by following the guide presented in Table 12.1.

Table 12.1 HTML Tags for Formatting Notes

Format	HTML Tag
Bold	\Bold\
Italics	\<i>Italics\</i>
Underline	\<u>Underline\</u>
~~Strikethrough~~	\<s>Strikethrough\</s>
Big size	\<big>Big size\</big>
Small size	\<small>Small size\</small>
Em dash like —	\—
Hyperlink to IdiotsGuides.com	\<a href="http://idiotsguides.com/"> IdiotsGuides.com\</a>
Bulleted (Unordered) list • Item • Item • Item • Item	\<ul> \<li>Item\</li> \<li>Item\</li> \<li>Item\</li> \<li>Item\</li> \</ul>
Numbered (Ordered) List 1. Step one 2. Step two 3. Step three 4. Step four	\<ol> \<li>Step one\</li> \<li>Step two\</li> \<li>Step three\</li> \<li>Step four\</li> \</ol>
Indented quote	\<blockquote>Indented quote \</blockquote>
# Heading 1	\<h1>Heading 1\</h1>
## Heading 2	\<h1>Heading 2\</h1>
### Heading 3	\<h1>Heading 3\</h1>

POKE

HTML tags come in two flavors—paired and unpaired. For paired tags, you type a tag where you want the formatting to begin and another tag where you want it to end; for example, <i>italics</i> displays *italics*. Unpaired codes stand alone, such as &mdash, which inserts an em dash that looks like this: —.

After composing your note, you can tag Facebook friends mentioned in the note or friends you want to make sure know about the note. To tag a friend, click in the **Tags** box, start typing your friend's name, and, when you see the name of the friend you want to tag, click it. Repeat the steps to tag other friends. After you post the note, Facebook automatically places a message on tagged friends' Walls about the existence of your note and sends them notifications (assuming they didn't disable notifications for notes).

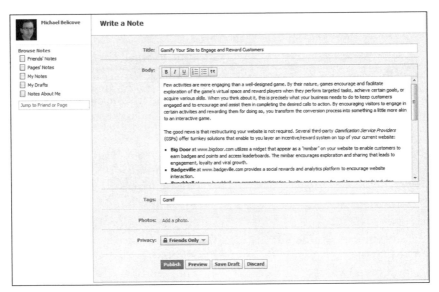

You can write a note.

Below the Body box are options to **Add a photo** (to upload a new photo or import a photo you previously uploaded). No surprises here, but if you need a refresher course on working with photos in Facebook, head back to Chapter 7.

Below the **Add a photo** option, you'll find the **Privacy** settings. Open the **Privacy** list and select the option that best represents the Facebook members you want to be able to access your note: **Everyone, Friends of Friends, Friends Only**, or **Customize**. The Customize option enables you to make the note visible to **Only Me** or cherry-pick individuals who can see the note; for example, you can click **Specific People** and choose specific individuals or a friend list.

When you're done composing your note and entering your privacy preferences, you have several options on how to proceed. Prior to publishing your post, we recommend that you click **Preview**, especially if you used any HTML tags to format your text. If everything looks fine, then you can publish it. If not, you can choose the option to edit the post. You also have the option to Save Draft (so you can complete the note and publish it later) or Discard to delete the note. When you're ready to publish it, click the **Publish** button.

Reviewing Your Notes

Assuming this is your first encounter with the Notes app, you don't have any notes to review; but since you're on the Notes page, let's talk about reviewing notes you posted. It's pretty easy—just click **Notes** (in the left menu) and then click **My Notes** below it. Notes you recently posted appear in reverse chronological order, and from here you can view the full note, change your privacy preferences, like the note, or add a comment. If you choose to view the full note, you can then edit it by clicking the **Edit** button (upper right).

You can also access your notes by heading to your Profile page and clicking **Notes** (in the left menu).

Finding Out Who's Talking About You

When posting a note, you and your friends have the option of tagging people mentioned in the note or those who might be interested in the note's content. Whenever a friend tags you in a note, you receive a notification, and the note appears in your Notes app and on your Wall. To view the note, click **Notes** (in the left menu) and then click **Notes About Me** under it. When you comment on a friend's note, it also appears on your My Notes page.

If you don't like what your friend has posted about you, or don't appreciate your friend tagging you in the note, you have two options:

- **Have your friend fix it:** Send your friend a message asking her to edit the note or remove the tag. This is usually the most prudent option because it educates your friend on what you think is acceptable. Your friend will know better next time.

- **Remove the tag:** To remove the tag, view the full note and then click **Remove my tag** (left column below the menus).

Feeding Blog Posts into Notes

If you already maintain a blog, posting to the blog and then reposting your entries in Facebook can be a royal hassle. To avoid doubling your workload, consider setting up an RSS feed in Facebook that automatically pulls entries from your existing blog to display them as Facebook Notes. Here's what you do:

1. Click **Profile** (in the top menu) and then click **Notes** (left menu).

2. Click the **+ Write a Note** button (upper right).

3. Click **My Notes** (left menu).

4. Click **Edit import settings** (left menu). The Import an External Blog page appears, prompting you to type the address of your website, blog, or RSS or Atom feed.

5. Click in the **Enter a website or RSS/Atom feed address** box and type the address of your blog or RSS or Atom feed, starting with **http://**.

6. Click the checkbox stating that you have the right to permit Facebook to reproduce the blog content.

7. Click **Start Importing**. Assuming everything works according to plan, Facebook displays a preview of the imported blog.

8. Check the preview, and if it looks okay, click **Confirm**. If it doesn't look okay, or you decide for whatever reason not to move forward with the import, click **Cancel**.

9. Click **Profile** and then **Notes** to view your newly imported blog posts.

If you decide later that you no longer want your blog entries to appear as notes, or you want to import entries from a different blog, you can remove the RSS feed. To do so, repeat steps 1 to 4 and then click **Stop Importing**. Facebook displays a confirmation indicating that your feed was successfully removed.

POKE

When you stop importing posts from a blog, this doesn't remove the blog entries that Facebook already imported. It simply prevents future blog entries from being added to your notes. However, you can delete individual notes: choose to view the full note, click the **Delete** link (above the comment box), and click **Confirm**.

Type the feed's address

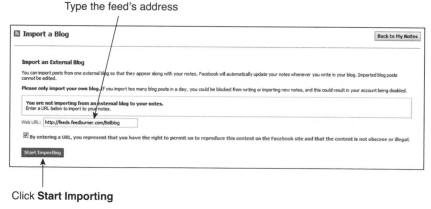

Click **Start Importing**

Import a blog.

The Least You Need to Know

- To launch the Notes app, head to your Home page, and then click **Notes** in the left menu.

- To share a friend's note by posting it to your News Feed and Wall, view the full note, click the **Share** link (above the comment box), type a brief explanation of why you think your friends will like this note, and then click the **Share** button.

- To post a note, click **Notes** (left menu), click the **+ Write a Note** button, complete the **Write a New Note** form, and click **Publish**.

- To find out whether you've been tagged in any notes, click **Notes** (in the left menu) and click **Notes About Me**.

- If you maintain a blog, you can set up an RSS feed to have Facebook automatically import your blog entries and publish them on your Notes page.

Harnessing the Power of Facebook Apps

Without its apps (applications), Facebook is the stripped-down model of a social-networking utility. All you'd have left is the Wall, News Feed, and some Profile data. Add in Facebook's core apps, and you get the fully loaded model, complete with photos, videos, Notes, Groups, Events, Messages, and Chat. All of these features are Facebook apps, which act sort of like plugins to make Facebook so feature-rich.

But there's more. Facebook and third-party developers provide even more apps to enhance Facebook, including apps to play games, use Facebook on your smartphone, share lists of your favorite books or movies, check your horoscope, send online greeting cards, and even get special deals from merchants when you "check in" to the business's Facebook Place using your smartphone. In this part, we reveal all you need to know to app up.

Exploring More Facebook Apps

In This Chapter

- Recognizing a Facebook app when you meet one
- Exploring Facebook's massive apps collection
- Dealing with app security and privacy issues
- Tweaking your Apps menu and bookmarks for easy app access
- Adjusting your Facebook app settings

Bet you didn't realize it, but you've already been using Facebook apps (applications). Photos, Video, Groups, Events, Notes, and Chat—they're all apps. These apps function as plugins for Facebook—accessories that enhance your experience. They add features that aren't part of the core Facebook experience (although a few select apps, like Photos and Notes, are part of the core experience).

In this chapter, we introduce you to app basics, reveal where you can find thousands of apps on Facebook, and show you how to gain quicker access to the apps you use.

Grasping the Basics of Facebook Apps

Facebook apps can help you do all sorts of things—from playing games to tracking birthdays and anniversaries and sharing movie reviews with friends. Facebook gives you access to thousands of apps, some its own creations but mostly those created by third-party developers. Later in this chapter, we show you how to search for specific apps and browse through Facebook's ever-growing collection of apps by category.

Fortunately, you have complete control over which apps you use. You can approve an app, block an app, or edit an app to control how it accesses and uses your information. If a friend invites you to use an app, you're entirely free to accept or reject the invitation.

In the following sections, we show you how to search for specific apps and browse Facebook's complete collection. We also explain some of the security issues surrounding apps and how to deal with them.

Digging Up More Apps

You're likely to discover plenty of apps through referrals as your friends recommend and invite you to use popular apps, especially games. If that doesn't satisfy your app-etite, you can explore Facebook to gather more fun and useful apps.

Facebook has a well-stocked library of apps, which you can browse or search at any time. To search for an app, click in the **Search** box (in the top menu), type one or two words to describe the type of app you're looking for, and press **Enter**. Facebook displays a bunch of stuff that matches your search criteria, which may include Groups, Pages, and even friends. Click **Applications** (in the left menu) to narrow the search results to only apps.

If more than 10 apps matched your description, you'll find a See More Results link below the search results, which you can click to see more apps that match your search word or phrase.

If you're not sure what you're looking for, head to your Home page and click **App Requests** (left menu). This displays the Apps page, which is divided into three sections. The top section shows any app requests you've received from friends. The next section shows any apps you're currently using. Finally, the Friends' Apps section shows a list of your friends, each followed by apps they've recently used.

Click **Apps**   Perform a search

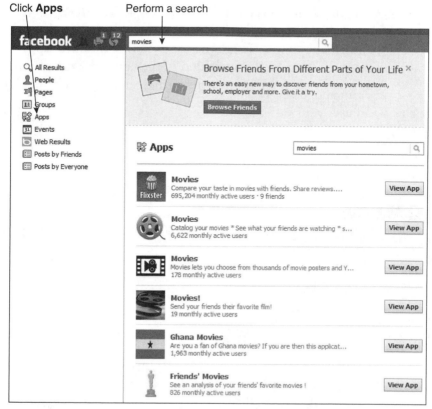

You can search for specific apps or types of apps.

To browse Facebook's App Directory, scroll to the bottom of the Apps page and click the **Apps Directory** link. The Apps Directory appears with a list of app categories (on the left), including Business, Education, and Entertainment. Click the desired category. A page appears that focuses on the category you chose. The main area of the page (in the middle) is divided into the following three sections:

- **Featured by Facebook:** Facebook recommends a couple apps in the selected category; you might want to check them out.

- **Apps You May Like:** These are some of the most popular apps in the selected category. Use the right-arrow button just above the list to flip to the next page of featured apps.

- **Category Name:** The third section simply lists the apps in the selected category, initially by popularity—most to least popular. You can rearrange the list to show the newest apps first by clicking **Recently Added** in the bar at the top of this section. To see more of the apps in this category, click **See All** (on the right end of the section bar).

Categories   Featured apps

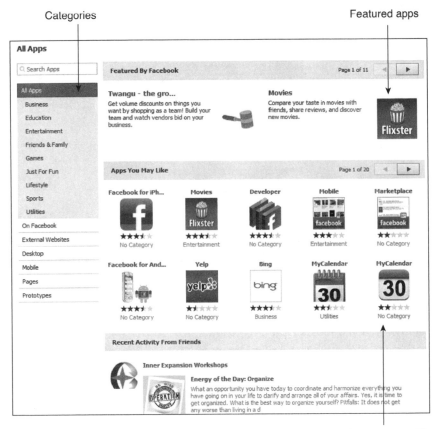

Apps you may like

Browse for apps by category.

Evaluating and Authorizing Apps

Authorizing an app is like taking on a new friend—you want to make sure you trust the new app before approving it. While most apps are trustworthy and harmless (in addition to being fun or useful), some may take liberties with information you allow it to access or even contact your Facebook friends on your behalf without your permission. So before you approve or authorize an app, do a background check to see what the app is all about and what other Facebook users have to say about it. (To control how much access apps have to your personal information, see Chapter 2.)

To perform a background check, head to the app's Page. (Every app has its own Page on Facebook.) To get to the Page, click the app in Facebook's Applications area or click the link for the app wherever you happen to see it—in an App Request, your News Feed, or the Allow Access? box that pops up if you choose later to accept the app.

The Information box on the left contains the app's star rating (with a top rating of five stars), the number of Facebook members using the app, and an indication of whether the app was developed by Facebook (most are not). On the right, you can see the number of your Facebook friends using the app along with each friend's Profile photo. (You may want to contact a friend who's using the app to find out more about it.)

Every app has its own Facebook Page.

To find out more about the app, you can click any of the options in the app's left menu to access Info, the app's Wall, Reviews, or whatever else the app developer has to share. On the app's Wall, you can usually read additional information about new features or tips for using the app. Assuming plenty of Facebook members are using the app and it has a strong rating, numerous endorsements, and no or very few serious complaints about it, it should be pretty trustworthy.

If you like what you see, click **Go to App** (near the top of the middle section of the app's Page) to start using the app. The Request for Permission page appears, letting you preview the type of information you'll be giving the app access to. You can also click links near the bottom of the box to check out the app's terms of service and privacy policy. To give the app permission and start using it, click **Allow**. To cancel, click the **Leave App** button.

When you authorize an app, Facebook creates a bookmark for it; bookmarked apps appear in the left menu in a separate section designated for your apps (just below the Groups section the last we checked). You may need to click the **More** link (below the section) to bring your apps into view. Click an app to access it.

POKE

Facebook automatically rearranges your bookmarked apps as you use them, listing the apps you use most frequently first.

Addressing Security Concerns

Even if you don't use third-party apps, some of your information could be exposed to them through your friends' use. Information that apps can access includes your name, networks, list of friends, personal information, education and work history, and any other Profile information you share with the public. To restrict access to your information, you can adjust your privacy settings for apps as explained in Chapter 2.

Responding to and Sending App Requests

As with most features on Facebook, apps are made to be shared. When a friend discovers an app she thinks is really cool (typically a game, a quiz, or a personality assessment), she shares it with her friends to encourage their participation. If a friend chooses to share an app with you, you receive an invitation that includes a brief description of the app.

To see whether you have any app requests, head to your Home page and click **App Requests** (left menu). (You may need to click the **More** link at the bottom of the Apps menu to bring the App Requests option into view.) The Apps page appears, displaying any app requests you've received, apps you already use, and Friends' Apps. To check for game requests, click **Games** (in the left menu).

In the following sections, you learn how to respond to an app request and send one of your own.

Responding to an App Request

When you receive an app request, the question for you is whether to authorize the app. You usually have the following three choices:

- **Click the App's link.** This displays the Request for Permission box, which describes the information the app needs to access in order to function. You can then click **Allow** or **Leave App**.

- **Click the Accept button.** App invitations always contain a button you can click to accept the invitation and authorize the app.

- **Click the X button.** You can click the **X** button to cancel the invitation without authorizing the app.

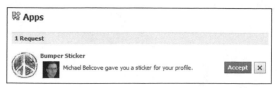

You can accept or ignore an app invitation.

You'll also see apps popping up on your News Feed or Live Feed, as a subtle invitation to participate. Assuming your friend hasn't disabled the News Feed and Wall notifications for apps, whenever he uses an app, a status update may appear in your News Feed and Live Feed indicating something related to your friend's interaction with the app. At the end of the post, you'll find the usual links to comment on the update or like it, along with another link to start using the app or some feature of it. Click the link to find out more about the app. Facebook displays some information about the app along with options to Allow or Leave App.

Inviting Your Friends to Use an Application

You just discovered the coolest app on the planet and are eager to share your good fortune with your friends ... or at least some of them. You could e-mail your friends to let them know, but Facebook offers an easier way—sending out app requests.

FRIEND-LY ADVICE

When it comes to sending app requests (or invitations), less is more. You may think FarmVille is the ultimate in social entertainment, but chances are pretty good that most of your friends would rather be doing something else. If you just can't help yourself, at least be selective in sending app requests. Send them only to friends you really think will appreciate them. If you choose to authorize an app and it prompts you to send invitations to friends, you can always click **Skip**.

To send an app request, head to the app's Page and click the tab for inviting friends; the tab name varies, so look for something like Invite or Friends. (Not all apps contain options for sending app requests.) Click the name or photo of each friend you want to invite. (You can also send invitations to non-Facebook members by typing their e-mail addresses in the Invite by E-Mail Address box.) After you've selected all the people you want to invite, click the **Send Request** button.

Editing and Removing Applications

Depending on the app you authorize, Facebook gives you some freedom to tweak the app's settings. For example, you can hide the Photos tab in your Profile, change the tab's privacy settings to limit access to it, or change the app's permissions to grant or revoke special privileges, such as sending you notifications or posting updates to your Wall.

To edit an app's settings, click **Account** (top menu) > **Privacy Settings**. Near the bottom of the page, below Apps and Websites, click **Edit Your Settings**. Next to Apps you use, click the **Edit Settings** button. This displays a list of apps you recently used. Next to the app whose settings you want to adjust, click **Edit Settings**. Settings appear for controlling the app's accessibility and permissions. These settings vary depending on the app; for example, you may be able to click **Remove** next to an option that enables the app to post updates to your Wall. Enter your preferences, and then click the **Close Section** button.

The app itself may offer additional settings via its interface. Look for an option labeled Settings or Profile Settings when you're using the app.

You can edit an app's settings to adjust its accessibility and permissions.

Some apps don't allow edits; however, you can remove any app you've added. To remove an app, click **Account** (top menu) > **Privacy Settings**. Near the bottom of the page, below Apps and Websites, click **Edit Your Settings**. Next to Apps you use, click the **Edit Settings** button. Next to the app you want to remove, click the **X** button.

> **FRIEND-LY ADVICE**
>
> If you're in the process of viewing or editing an app's settings, you can remove the app by clicking the **Remove app** link (to the upper right of the app's settings).

The Least You Need to Know

- You can access Facebook's core apps via the left menu.
- To search for apps, click in the **Search** box (top menu), type your search word or phrase, press **Enter**, and then click **Apps** (in the left menu).
- To browse for apps, click **App Requests** (left menu), and then scroll down and click **Apps Directory**.
- To access one of your apps, click its bookmark (left menu) or click **App Requests** and then select the app from your Apps page.
- Before authorizing an app, research its Facebook Page to find out what other Facebook members have said about it.
- If you receive an app request from a friend, you may accept or reject it.
- To tweak an app's settings, click **Account > Privacy Settings**, scroll down below Apps and Websites, click **Edit your settings**, click **Edit Settings** (next to Apps you use), click **Edit Settings** next to the app you want to edit, and use the resulting options to enter your preferences.

Playing Games with Friends and Strangers

In This Chapter

- Checking out the top games on Facebook
- Finding even more games to play
- Convincing friends to join in the fun
- Making new friends through games

A lot of people waste ... er ... *spend* a lot of time on Facebook playing all sorts of games, voting in polls, and taking personality tests like "Which flower represents you?" and "Which dead rock star are you?"

If you enjoy sharing in the revelry, this chapter introduces you to some of the most popular games and other distractions on Facebook, shows you how to find even more games and add them to your list of favorites, and explains how to engage others in a friendly game of whatever it is you enjoy playing. Games can be a great way to meet new friends and break the ice.

Oh, the Games People Play!

Social games on Facebook are all the rage, but different games appeal to different people. In addition, the popularity of certain games tends to rise and fall. When poker was all the rage, Texas Hold'Em Poker was one of the most popular games on Facebook, followed closely by Mafia Wars. After some time, however, people began leaving the card table for FarmVille, where they could manage their own virtual farms in cyberspace.

In the following list, you get to sample the games that made the top-10 list while we were writing the book. We'd wager that by the time you read this, some of these games won't make the cut, and new games will have risen to the top, but these top popular options give you a pretty good feel for the cross-section of social games available on Facebook:

1. **CityVille:** In CityVille, you build a city from the ground up by growing crops and supplying produce to stores and restaurants. As your city grows, you build houses, collect rent, create businesses, expand into other cities with franchise operations, erect community buildings, exchange goods, and manage finances in the hopes of becoming Mayor of your fair city.

2. **FarmVille:** In FarmVille, you till the soil, plant seeds and trees, harvest cash crops, build farmhouses and barns, milk cows, decorate, expand your farm, and even invest in farm machinery to make your job easier. Invite your Facebook friends to settle on neighboring farmland, and you can help them with their farms to earn extra cash. If you get serious about this farming thing, you can pay real cash to buy game money that'll help you build your farm faster.

3. **Texas Hold'Em Poker:** Zynga's popular poker game allows you to ante up with your friends and engage in one of the classic games of all time … Texas style. You start each day with a small stack of chips plus any winnings you have accumulated from previous games. If you have a credit card handy, you can purchase more chips, or you can sign up for offers from companies to receive free chips. Unfortunately, you can't cash out that $5 million you won the night before.

4. **FrontierVille:** If you're tired of technology, you can turn back the clock and head west to establish a home in the wilderness and raise a family. Along the way, you're challenged to accomplish never-ending goals, including clearing the land, planting crops, chopping wood, erecting buildings, getting married, clobbering dangerous animals, and helping your neighbors.

5. **Café World:** In Café World, you become the chef of your own restaurant. You start out with about $2,000, four stoves, three food counters, some chairs and tables, and a door through which your future customers will enter. You hire a waiter, select foods to cook and serve, and then start cooking. Some foods take longer to cook than others, so timing is key. You need to make sure you don't burn anything and that you have enough customers to serve before the food gets cold.

6. **Mafia Wars:** Mafia Wars is the flip side of CityVille. Instead of running honest businesses and contributing positively to your community, you start a mafia family with your friends, run a criminal empire, vie for respect, and fight to become the most powerful family in New York City. After reaching certain levels in the game, you get to travel to Cuba and Russia to increase your power and reach. You earn money and power by doing jobs and robbing other mafia organizations.

7. **Bejeweled Blitz:** This addictive video game displays a grid of different-colored gems and challenges players to rearrange them to line up three of the same gems in a row. Every time you line up three gems in a row, they disappear, and you score points. The game offers several ways to score bonus points, including a speed multiplier, power gems (when you align four in a row) that you can use to destroy the nine gems around it, and a hyper gem (when you align five in a row) that you can use to destroy all the gems of one color.

8. **Pet Society:** In the world of Pet Society, you create your own virtual pet and then try to keep it happy by providing food, water, and treats; petting and grooming it; engaging in interesting outings and activities; furnishing its home; and competing in contests. Because this is a society, you get to meet and mingle with other pets as you explore this virtual world of pets.

9. **Ravenwood Fair:** In Ravenwood Fair, your task is to transform a scary forest into a beautiful fair, complete with fun and games. In the process of clearing the forest of brambles, stones, and spooky trees, you discover old, abandoned games, buildings, and décor to use in building your fair.

10. **Treasure Isle:** Few activities are more engaging than a good treasure hunt. In Treasure Isle, you become an adventurer and have the opportunity to dig for rare and valuable treasure with your friends. You have a limited amount of time and energy, so you need to work quickly and efficiently to dig up all of the treasures that complete a set ... or trade duplicate treasures with friends.

Plant and harvest virtual crops in FarmVille.

Finding Games on Facebook

Tracking down games on Facebook is as easy as tracking down apps, as explained in Chapter 13. In fact, games are apps. Although you can use the Search box in the top menu to perform a broad search for games, you're usually better off browsing Facebook's collection. To start browsing, head to your Home page and click **Games** (in the left menu; you may need to click **More** at the bottom of the menu to bring it into view). This takes you to the Games page, which is divided into the following areas:

- **Game Stories:** If you play a game, you can share stories about challenges and progress in those games with friends who also play the game, without bothering friends who don't play the game. If you play any games, you and your friends' stories about those games appear here.

- **Your Games:** Icons for any Facebook games you play appear in this section, providing you with quick access to those games.

- **Friends' Games:** If your friends play games on Facebook, those games appear in this section. Choosing a game that one of your friends already plays makes finding a playmate easier.

- **Games Directory:** At the very bottom is a link to access the Games Directory. Click the **Games Directory** link to view games featured by Facebook, games you might like, and a list of the most popular games.

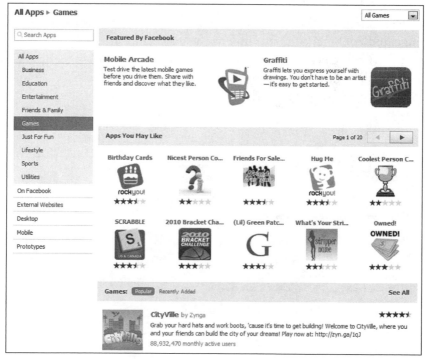

Browse the Games Directory to find games.

Let's Play Already!

Every game is unique, so providing instructions on how to play each one would be ridiculous. All we have room to cover are the basics— launching the game, inviting friends to play, and responding to invitations from friends.

> **POKE**
>
> Unfortunately, game developers typically provide little or no guidance for new players to get up and running. You pretty much have to start playing and hope that on-the-job training is sufficient. You might be able to pick up a little guidance on the game's page. Just click the game's name wherever it appears as a link. If you have friends who've played the game, you can consult them. You can also search the web for instructions—sometimes players post basic instructions on sites such as eHow.com or the game's developer offers a beginner's guide.

Launching a Game

Whenever you authorize a game, Facebook adds it to your Games page and bookmarks it, so a link to the game appears in the left menu. When you're ready to play, click the game's bookmark or click **Games** (left menu) and then click the game you want to play. (Your games appear at the top of the list.)

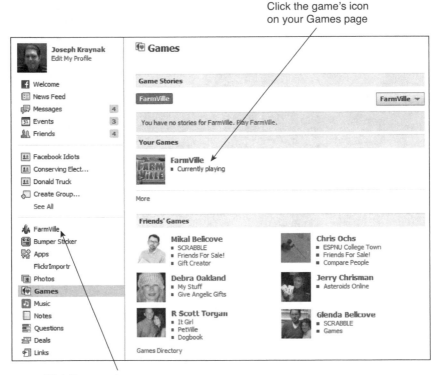

Click the game's icon on your Games page

Click the game's bookmark

To play a game, click its name in the left menu or on the Games page.

Encouraging Your Friends to Play

The main purpose of social games is to socialize, so almost every game on Facebook is geared to engage friends in the fun. FarmVille, for example, constantly encourages players to spread the word and invite friends to play. The invitation can be something soft, such as posting a story, or something more direct, like asking your friends to help you find a home for the new kitten that just wandered onto your property. You can also invite friends at any time by clicking **Invite Friends**. If your friends are already FarmVille players, click **Add Neighbors** to make them your neighbors.

However you choose to invite friends to play, an Invite Friends page pops up, prompting you to select from your list of friends. Click the friends you want to invite and click the button to send your invitation(s).

You can invite friends to join in the fun.

WHOA!

Avoid the temptation to invite all of your friends to play the cool new game you just discovered. Invite only those friends you know enjoy playing games, and from that subset, select only the friends you strongly feel will enjoy playing *this* game. Invite the wrong person too many times, and she's likely to either block your future invitations or de-friend you.

Making New Friends Through Games

If you're having trouble finding friends to play your favorite game with you, consider joining a group devoted to the game. Check out Chapter 9 to learn more about groups and how to find and join groups. You're likely to find several groups packed with people eager to meet new players. In addition, your new friends can help bring you up to speed on the game and provide useful tips.

Responding to a Friend's Request to Play

If someone sends you an invitation to play a game, you should see a Game Requests link in the left menu. Click **Game Requests** to access your Games page. You can then click the game's name to find out more about it or click **Accept** to accept the invitation or **X** (the Hide button) to ignore it.

If you hide the invitation, Facebook gives you two more options. You can block the game, so you never receive invitations from any-one to play this particular game, or you can ignore all requests from the person who sent you the invitation, so you never receive another invitation from this person to play a game or use an app. (You can undo this at any time by adjusting your privacy settings, as explained in Chapter 2.)

The Least You Need to Know

- Facebook games are social games, designed for group interaction.
- Some of the more popular Facebook games include CityVille, FarmVille, Mafia Wars, and Texas Hold'Em Poker.
- To find games, head to your Home page and click **Games** (in the left menu), and then scroll down to the bottom of the Games page and click **Games Directory**.
- After authorizing a game, you can find it on your Games page.
- Be selective when inviting friends to play games. Not all of your friends will appreciate receiving game invitations.

Facebooking with Your Mobile Phone

Chapter

15

In This Chapter

- Using a smartphone app to access Facebook
- Setting up Facebook Mobile on your phone
- Receiving and sending status updates remotely
- Uploading digital photos and video clips from your phone
- Checking in to Places and getting Deals

When you leave your home or office or wherever it is you usually spend time on Facebook, you don't have to leave your friends behind. In fact, you might find that using Facebook on your mobile phone is actually more useful and convenient than on your laptop or desktop computer. Think about it; many of today's cell phones have built-in photo, video, and text capabilities, which is exactly why most people use Facebook—to share photos, status updates, and videos. Why wait until you're in front of your computer when you can do all of that and more right from your Internet-enabled phone?

Assuming you have a cell phone, iPhone, Android device, BlackBerry, Palm, or other such wireless gadget, you can update your status, view and upload photos and videos, check your Facebook messages, check in at businesses and locations you visit, and more. This chapter takes you on the road with your mobile phone and shows you how to join the 250 million people who access Facebook using their mobile devices.

Accessing Facebook with a Smartphone App

For the majority of us who use a smartphone (think iPhone, BlackBerry, Palm, Android device, and so on), the Facebook experience is only as good as the smartphone's app. And while we all want the same user experience and interface we enjoy on our desktop computers to appear on our smartphone, well ... that just isn't possible. Aside from the fact that phone screens are at best ⅛ the size of the smallest desktop monitor or power user's laptop screen, there's the whole issue of bandwidth and connectivity, both of which dictate that the user experience on a smartphone is going to be, well, different.

Whether you use an iPhone, BlackBerry, Palm, Android device, or nearly any other type of smartphone, device-specific apps are available for you to connect with and enjoy Facebook from the palm of your hand. Each device has app stores where you can download your device's Facebook app. To get started, visit the app store associated with your mobile phone and search for "Facebook." Once you find your device-specific app, follow the on-screen instructions for downloading the app to your phone.

FRIEND-LY ADVICE

While many of today's smartphones come with a preinstalled Facebook app, some may not. iPhone users can access the Apple App Store via iTunes on a desktop or laptop computer. BlackBerry's app store can be found at www.blackberry.com. If you use a Palm device, visit www.hpwebos.com to find your Facebook app. If your phone runs the Android operating system, visit market.android.com for your phone's Facebook app. And if you use a different type of mobile phone, visit m.fb.snaptu.com/f from your cell phone (once there, you'll find a Facebook-specific app for nearly any other mobile phone). In each case, the app is free and simple to download and use.

Setting Up Facebook Mobile

If you're old school and prefer to skip using an app to access Facebook, the first thing you need to do is log in to your Facebook account using your computer and type **Mobile** in the Search box, or visit www.facebook.com/mobile. Once there, you'll see numerous options, including information about uploading photos via e-mail, updating your status from your phone via text messaging, receiving News Feed items on your phone, and downloading a Facebook app built specifically for mobile phones. While all of these are interesting and useful, what you want to focus on right now is the **Edit Settings** link at the bottom of the page.

> **FRIEND-LY ADVICE**
>
> Make sure your cell phone is web-enabled. If you can browse the World Wide Web and send and receive text messages using your phone, you're all set. If, however, your cell phone isn't web-enabled or set up to send and receive text messages, you'll need to consult your wireless carrier about switching to a phone that allows you to use Facebook.

Clicking on the **Edit Settings** link brings you to the Mobile tab of your Account Settings, where you can register your mobile phone for Facebook Text Messages, which include status updates, Wall posts, messages sent to friends' Inboxes, and more. Follow these steps to get started:

1. Click **Register for Facebook Text Messages**, which opens a pop-up window asking you to choose your country and mobile service provider. (While most mobile providers support Facebook, some don't. If yours isn't on the list, Facebook Mobile won't work on your phone.)

2. Click the **Next** button and follow the on-screen instructions to send a text message containing only the letter "F" (without quotes) to 32665 (FBOOK).

3. Click the **Next** button, and then check your cell phone for a text message from Facebook containing your unique Facebook Mobile Activation Code.

4. Enter your Facebook Mobile Activation Code in the designated space.

5. Make sure the **Add my cell number to my Profile** option is clicked.

6. Click **Confirm**.

That's it. Your mobile phone is now activated to use Facebook Mobile, and you're ready to roll. Now you're all set to start receiving status updates. To designate a friend or Page you want to receive status updates from via your mobile phone, visit the **Mobile** tab under **Account Settings**, and enter the name of the friend or Page under **Whose status updates should go to my phone?**. (For more about Facebook Pages, see Chapter 17.)

Of course, Facebook Mobile enables you to do more than simply receive status updates. You can now post status updates, share photos and videos, send and receive Facebook messages, receive Wall posts, and use third-party applications that enhance your Facebook experience and productivity. Keep reading to tap the full potential of Facebook Mobile.

WHOA!

While Facebook doesn't charge for status updates, Wall posts, and messages, your mobile service provider does. Check your mobile rate plan before signing up to send messages and receive all your friends' status updates as text messages on your phone. As you'll see later in this chapter, if you're not on one of those all-inclusive plans, you may be better off using Facebook via your phone's web browser, if it's equipped with one.

Texting to Facebook

After you've activated your phone to send and receive Facebook status updates, Wall posts, and messages, performing those tasks is pretty easy. (And if you stop and think about it, posting status updates when you're out and about, when you're experiencing life and have more to say or sitting around twiddling your thumbs in a waiting room or airport, makes a lot more sense, too.) Most Facebook users don't post status updates only when they're sitting in front of their computers. We can't tell you how many times we've found the need—okay, it's really more of a *desire* than a need—to post status updates on the road, in the passenger seat of the car, at a restaurant waiting for a friend, sitting in the airport, or at a game where the most amazing thing just happened.

Having the flexibility to share interesting news, opinions, and observations with our Facebook friends whenever and wherever the spirit moves us is a real treat. Some business owners and leaders have come to consider it a necessity. In the following sections, we show you how to use Facebook Mobile to access Facebook's most popular features when you're away from your computer.

Posting Status Updates

Using your mobile phone to keep your Facebook friends—and fans, if you use Facebook for your business, organization, or brand—updated on what you're thinking or up to is a snap. Once you've authorized your cell phone for Facebook Mobile, posting status updates from your phone is as simple as sending an SMS (short message service) to 32665 (FBOOK). Said differently, text a message—for example, "I'm reading *The Complete Idiot's Guide to Facebook*; you should, too!"—from your Facebook-enabled cell phone to 32665 and it will show up in your Facebook account as a status update.

But wait, there's more.

Texting Facebook Commands

Now that your phone is set up to send and receive messages from Facebook, you can do any of the following activities:

- **Send a message to a Facebook friend:** Text **msg** followed by your friend's name followed by your message to 32665, and your text shows up in your friend's Inbox on Facebook. For example, "msg joseph kraynak running 45 min late."

- **Search for a friend's Facebook details:** Text **search [name]** to 32665, and you receive a text message from Facebook containing your friend's Facebook data, which usually includes at least a phone number and e-mail address. For example, "search Mikal Belicove" will result in receiving a message with Mikal's publicly available information on Facebook (assuming he's your friend).

- **Post a note on Facebook:** Text **note** followed by your note's content to 32665 and your note appears on Facebook and in your News Feed.

- **Post a message on a friend's Wall:** Text **wall** followed by your friend's name followed by your Wall post to 32665, and your message appears on your friend's Facebook Wall. For example, "wall Mikal Belicove Really enjoying *The Complete Idiot's Guide to Facebook*. Nicely done!"

- **Send a friend request:** Text **add** followed by your future Facebook friend's name to 32665 to send a friend request. For example, text "add Mikal Belicove" to send Mikal a friend request.

- **Become a fan:** Text **fan** followed by the name of the Facebook fan page to 32665 to instantly become a fan of a specific Page on Facebook. For example, text "fan Idiot Book" to become a fan of our official Page for the book.

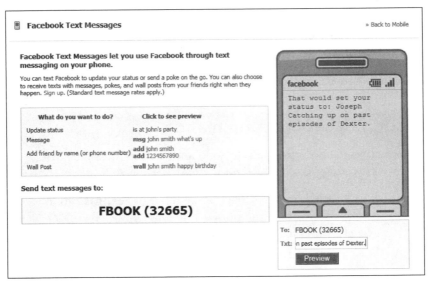

Facebook's text messaging simulator enables you to take text messaging for a test drive online.

As you can see, Facebook goes to great lengths to make it as easy as possible to get the most out of your Facebook text messaging experience. Using an online text message simulator, you can see what type of text messages you can send and receive using your Facebook-enabled cell phone. To access the simulator, head to www.facebook.com/mobile/?texts.

Uploading Photos and Videos from Your Phone

With a photo- or video-enabled cell phone and access to your own unique Facebook e-mail address, you no longer need to download photos or videos to your home computer or laptop and then go through the steps outlined in Chapters 7 and 8 to upload them to Facebook. With Facebook Mobile, you simply shoot your photos and videos on your phone and upload them to Facebook via e-mail whenever you want.

To get started, locate and add your personalized Facebook e-mail address for mobile uploads. Here's how:

1. Click the **Mobile** link on the bottom of any Facebook Page.

2. Look for the section titled **Upload via E-mail**. Here you'll find your personalized e-mail address for sending photos and videos to your Facebook Profile.

3. Copy and paste the e-mail address into your cell phone's e-mail program or text messaging address book and you're good to go. Or click the **Send me my upload e-mail** button to have Facebook text the address to your cell phone.

You can now easily upload to Facebook from your cell phone by sending your photos and videos to your personalized Facebook e-mail address.

FRIEND-LY ADVICE

You can also use your personalized e-mail address for mobile uploads to upload photos and videos from your laptop or desktop computer. Simply attach your photos or videos to an outgoing e-mail message and send it to your personalized upload e-mail address as explained previously.

When you upload via e-mail, whatever you type into your message's subject line automatically becomes the title of the video or the caption of the photo you're uploading.

After you've uploaded your photos or videos to Facebook, the uploaded items are automatically posted to your Profile. Photos show up in your Mobile Uploads album, which is accessible via your Photos tab, and video files are stored on your Video tab. We recommend editing uploaded photos and videos the next time you log in to Facebook, because the only content set for Mobile Uploads is the caption for photos and title for videos. See Chapter 7 for more on editing photos and Chapter 8 for information on editing videos.

Taking Facebook Mobile Web on the Road

If your cell phone can access the Internet and has a web browser, check out m.facebook.com from your phone's browser. Here you'll find Facebook Mobile Web, a version of Facebook that's optimized for cell phones with web browser capabilities.

If you're skeptical about how Facebook will look on a screen $\frac{1}{8}$ the size of a standard computer screen, we don't blame you. To help you overcome your skepticism, Facebook has built a nifty Mobile Web simulator that lets you see what your Profile, Inbox, photos, and more will look like from a web-enabled cell phone using your laptop or desktop computer. Visit www.facebook.com/mobile/?web to take Facebook Mobile Web for a spin.

Most web-enabled cell phones allow you to access your Facebook Profile just as you would from your laptop or desktop computer. Some differences do exist, however, so you'll want to download the version that's made for your cell phone and see which features work for you and your on-the-go Facebook needs.

FRIEND-LY ADVICE

Facebook Mobile can even save you money. With Facebook Places and Deals, discussed in Chapter 19, businesses you frequent and follow on Facebook may notify you when you're in their neighborhood and offer you special deals on food, beverages, clothing, and more!

Take Facebook Mobile Web for a spin with the simulator.

Checking in with Facebook Places

When you're on the go, you may want to let your friends know where you are and what you're doing ... and find out where they are and what they're doing. That's now possible with Facebook Places— a locations-based feature that lets you check in wherever you happen to be and tag any Facebook friends you're with. You may even want to engage in locations-based games with friends and other Facebook members.

In addition, if you permit them, nearby businesses can access information about your whereabouts and offer you special deals. Imagine strolling through the mall at lunchtime and receiving a two-for-one deal from the restaurant where you want to dine or a 25 percent off coupon from a store you just happen to be planning to shop at!

FRIEND-LY ADVICE

If you want to use Facebook Places as a locations-based marketing tool for your business, check out Chapter 19, where you'll also learn about Facebook Deals.

Getting Started

To start using the Places feature, you need a smartphone (such as iPhone, Android, or BlackBerry) equipped with its up-to-date Facebook app. Another option is to access the Places app through your mobile device's web browser by going to touch.facebook.com. You must be using a browser that supports HTML 5 and geolocation. (You should be able to use Places from a portable computer as well, but at the time we wrote this, you could access Places via computer but accomplish very little once you got there.)

After logging in using your mobile device's Facebook app, click or tap the **Places** tab. The location of the tab varies according to the app or browser you're using. You may need to click **More** to bring the tab into view.

On the Places page, you'll see where your friends have recently checked in and any of your own recent check-ins. You can tap or click a friend's check-in to access additional details about places they've checked in to, including location, description, directions, comments, and check-ins from other friends at that location.

Checking In

After reaching Places, you can check in to let Facebook know where you are. Click the **Check In** button. The first time you choose to check in, Facebook displays a message indicating that it wants to track your physical location. To allow Facebook to track your physical location, click **Allow**. If you changed your mind and really don't want Facebook tracking you, click **Deny**. Assuming you clicked **Allow**, you're now greeted by the Places interface, where you can share your location with friends, find out where they are, and tag any friends who are with you.

When prompted to share your location, click or tap the link to share where you are with friends. A list of available nearby locations appears. If the place you're checking in to isn't shown, click or tap the right-arrow button near the Places tab to find more nearby locations. If you still can't find it, choose **Add** and enter a name and description of the place.

After sharing your location, a Place page appears, showing a map of where the place is located, a list of friends and other Facebook members currently checked in there (if any), and a Friend Activity stream from and about friends who've been there. You can now post an update on what you're doing there or tag friends who are with you.

WHOA!

Tag your friends before checking in. You may not be able to tag them afterward.

Adjusting Your Places Privacy Settings

By default, only your friends can see the places you've checked in to. To change the setting, click **Account > Privacy Settings**, and then the **Customize settings** link. Click the button next to places you check in to and choose the desired setting: **Everyone, Friends of Friends**, or **Friends Only**, or click **Customize**, enter your preferences, and click **Save Setting**.

If you'd like to keep nearby friends notified of your whereabouts, click **Enable** next to Include me in "People Here Now" after I check in.

By default, your Facebook friends can check you in to places, which could be a dangerous thing if you're somewhere you're not supposed to be, doing something you're not supposed to do, or you have friends who like to mess with you. To prevent friends from checking you in, click the **Edit Settings** button next to Friends can check me in to Places and choose **Disabled**. For more about privacy settings, flip back to Chapter 2.

Taking Advantage of Check-In Deals

Now you have an even better reason for using Facebook—Check-in Deals! Businesses can offer deals based on your current location as specified in Facebook Places. These deals are open to anyone who checks in to the place of the business that's offering the deal.

Businesses offer deals to attract more customers, retain existing customers, and generate sales without the hassle of printed coupons. You simply pull up the deal on your mobile display and show it to the person who's serving you.

The following sections tell you how to start taking advantage of Check-in Deals. If you own a business and want to offer Check-in Deals, skip to Chapter 19 to learn how.

> **FRIEND-LY ADVICE**
>
> Facebook draws a distinction between Daily Deals and Check-in Deals. Daily Deals are coupons that consumers may purchase online; for example, two wave runner rentals for $60 instead of $120 or an eight-week improvisational comedy course that normally costs $150 for $100. Check-in Deals are free for the cost of checking in to a business's Facebook Place. Here we talk about Check-in Deals. See Chapter 19 for more about Daily Deals.

Finding Check-In Deals

To find Check-in Deals for a local establishment, use your mobile device to access Facebook's Places, click the place where you plan to do business, and click **Deals** (left menu). You may also discover Check-in Deals outside of Places that your friends choose to share on their Wall or your Wall, in a group, or via a private message.

When you see a deal that interests you, click it for more information about it, including when the deal starts and ends, what you need to do to earn the deal, and how to go about claiming the deal—this usually consists of pulling up the deal on your smartphone and showing it to the person who's serving you.

What you need to do to earn a deal depends on the type of deal—Individual, Friends, Loyalty, Charity. For Individual and Charity Deals, you don't need to do anything. Individual Deals are usually discounts that any Facebook members are eligible for simply by liking a place/Page or checking in to a place. With Charity Deals, the business makes a donation to a charity of its choice when you make a purchase. Eligibility for a Friends Deal hinges on whether you get a certain number of friends (from 1 to 8) to check in with you. To earn a Loyalty Deal, you need to check in to the business's Facebook Place the specified number of times (2 to 20).

Sharing Deals with Your Friends

When you stumble upon a great deal, you may want to let your friends in on it. To share a deal, here's what you do:

1. Click the **Share** link for the Check-in Deal.

2. Open the **Share** drop-down menu and specify how you want to share the deal: **On your own Wall**, **On a friend's Wall**, **In a group**, or **In a private message**.

3. If you chose to share on your friend's Wall, in a group, or in a private message, enter the name of the friend(s) or group(s).

4. (Optional) Type a brief introduction to the deal, such as why you think your friend would appreciate it.

5. Click the **Share Deal** button.

The Least You Need to Know

- Most smartphones have a Facebook app that makes accessing the site fun and easy. Visit your phone's app store to find the Facebook app best suited for your phone.

- To set up Facebook Mobile for your cell phone, head to www. facebook.com/mobile, click **Edit Settings**, and follow the on-screen instructions.

- To post a status update from your cell phone, send a text message to 32665 (FBOOK).

- To post a message on a friend's Wall, text **wall** followed by your friend's name followed by your Wall post to 32665.

- To obtain a personalized Facebook e-mail address for mobile uploads, go to www.facebook.com/mobile.

- To access Facebook Places, log in to Facebook using your mobile phone's Facebook app or browser and click the **Places** tab.

- To find Check-in Deals, access the Facebook Place of the business and click **Deals** (in the left menu).

Getting Down to Business on Facebook

Doing business on Facebook is sort of like selling raffle tickets at a family reunion. People gather on Facebook to socialize, not to buy stuff, and they don't appreciate being blasted with ads or sales pitches. Yet most Facebook users expect businesses and organizations to have a presence in the community and provide something engaging and beneficial—typically valuable, relevant information and maybe special offers.

In this part, we try to sell you on the idea of doing business on Facebook, and we show you how to use Facebook's advertising features to do business in a way that can lift sales, increase customer retention, and attract new customers without turning off the people you're trying to impress.

Doing Business in a Social Setting

In This Chapter

- Recognizing the business potential of Facebook
- Incorporating Facebook advertising in your marketing campaign
- Getting customers involved with groups
- Avoiding the most common pitfalls

Selling effectively in a social setting requires a huge paradigm shift from traditional marketing, advertising, and sales. On Facebook and other social-networking sites, establishing credibility and trust and building relationships take precedence over making a sale. Companies and brands that succeed are rewarded through positive word-of-mouth advertising and referrals. Those who ruffle the feathers of too many Facebook members feel their wrath as the negative publicity spreads almost instantly.

In this chapter, we make the case for implementing Facebook in your promotional efforts, introduce you to features designed specifically for this purpose, and provide tips on how to do business most effectively on Facebook.

The Business Case for Facebook

If we told you 620,000,000+ people were happily gathered in one central location online—many of whom are your customers and prospective customers—and that the majority of them expect to see your business or brand there, wouldn't you want to be there, too? In a nutshell, that's the case for promoting your business or brand on Facebook. With hundreds of millions of consumers using this one über–social networking platform to connect with friends and interact with others around topics that interest them, your business has a tremendous opportunity to gain powerful access to the very people who fill your coffers.

Unlike banner, e-mail, and pay-per-click advertising (push-marketing tactics, in which you push your message to the masses and wait for a direct response), setting up shop for your business on Facebook is a highly effective pull strategy. When done correctly, it enables you to engage with your customers—and engagement is what Facebook is all about.

With engagement comes the possibility of word-of-mouth advertising, which, of course, is nothing new. What is new is that the Internet has become the breeding ground for the placement and distribution of user-generated content—and not just the funny sound your cat just made. Users talk about businesses and products, ask and answer questions, post and read reviews, share rip-off stories about bad experiences they've had with certain companies, and sing the praises of top-notch businesses and quality brands.

Facebook expands the reach of word-of-mouth advertising and increases the speed at which it spreads, and it has quickly become the platform of choice for businesses and their customers to connect and engage online. Regardless of whether your business has a presence on Facebook, chances are that your customers do, so you should be there, too.

FRIEND-LY ADVICE

At the end of the day, marketing on Facebook is still marketing, so don't abandon everything you already know about marketing. You simply need to know how to apply your marketing savvy and expertise to Facebook.

Tapping the Power of Facebook Advertising

Most users know that businesses and organizations can advertise on Facebook. Glance at the right side of nearly any Facebook Page and you'll see at least one ad. What many businesses and organizations fail to realize, however, is that several of Facebook's advertising features are free. In the following sections, we introduce you to both the free and paid advertising offerings and reveal how you can use them alone or together to rev up your promotional efforts on Facebook.

Launching a Facebook Page

Every business needs a home, and on Facebook the home of choice for a business or brand is its Facebook Page. Pages are meant for businesses and brands to share news, opinions, and information about their products and services with Facebook members. Packed with available features that enable your business to engage with fans (members who choose to like your Page), Facebook Pages enable you to build relationships, which have the potential to lead to positive word-of-mouth advertising and brand evangelism.

By posting timely and clever status updates, which show up in members' News Feeds, businesses on Facebook find they're able to keep customers and prospects well informed of company news, events, contests, special offers, and more, as well as drive traffic back to their websites.

Before Facebook, if you wanted to reach out to customers to inform them of, say, a contest, you relied on e-mail or newsletters, which many people find more annoying than engaging. With a Facebook Page, a business can post a status update announcing a promotion, and chances are fairly good that a fan will leave a comment, which can spark a chain reaction. The comment gets published in the fan's News Feed for all his friends to see and inspires other Facebook members to respond with their own comments, which in turn further promotes the promotion.

If you're a business owner or marketing manager focused on your return on investment (ROI) from engaging with customers and others (which we like to refer to as ROE—return on engagement), you'll be glad to know that Facebook Pages come complete with a suite of free tools that enable you to measure how many fans interact with your Page, how old they are, where they live, and more.

In short, if you have something to promote, build a Page. We show you how in Chapter 17.

Cross-Promoting Facebook on Your Blog or Website

Facebook presents the classic "if you build it, will they come" conundrum. On the one hand, your customers or brand advocates may think to search for you on Facebook, and if they do happen to find your Page, they're likely to become fans. On the other hand, while the majority of Facebook members expect your business or organization to have a presence on Facebook, they rarely, if ever, search for you. Rather, they affiliate because of something you've done to inform them of your Facebook Page, like posting a "find us on Facebook" badge on your website or blog or sending a special e-mail message to them announcing your new Facebook Page. (In Chapter 17, we show you how to create a badge for your Page.)

Cross-promotion is crucial to building a fan base on Facebook. Take every opportunity to let your customers know about your Facebook Page and why they should want to become fans. If you run a retail storefront, restaurant, or office, print some postcards or small fliers announcing your Facebook address, and make sure everyone receives one on their way out the door. Add a Facebook badge to your company e-newsletter, all of your e-mail marketing communications, and, of course, your website and blog. Heck, you might even go so far as to print your Facebook address on the company letterhead! If it works, go for it. Do anything you can to build a following on Facebook.

Posting Ads on Facebook

If all this "engagement" stuff has got you scratching your head and wondering whether you can just post an ad on Facebook promoting your products or services, then Facebook ads are for you. With 620,000,000+ active users, all of whom have supplied Facebook with their geographic and demographic information, Facebook ads allow you to reach only the people you want to target.

Suppose you're a wedding photographer and you only want to target your ad toward women between the ages of 24 and 30 in a certain locale whose relationship status is Engaged. Well, on Facebook, you can. Similarly, if you own the hip new sushi restaurant in town, you can target your ads toward a specific demographic, and if you run a Colorado-based not-for-profit that takes high school kids on back-country trips, you can target local or national wilderness enthusiasts to make a donation to your cause.

To learn more about Facebook ads, check out Chapter 18.

Going Viral with Facebook for Websites

Through status updates, notes, photos, videos, and more, your business can create quite an impressive presence on Facebook. But what if you're BlackPast.org, the Google of African American History, with 4,000 pages of content crying out to be shared with Facebook fans?

Copying and pasting all that content into individual notes or attempting to create a status update calling attention to each one of your web pages would be a nightmare, even for an intern! The solution to your problem (actually, more opportunity than problem) may be found in Facebook for Websites.

Think of Facebook for Websites as a programming tool that enables your website programmer to add certain Facebook features—like Share, Comment, Recent Friend Activity, and more—to your website. So in the preceding example, BlackPast.org can add Facebook's Share button to each of its 4,000 or so pages, which encourages its visitors to recommend the content to all their Facebook friends.

There's a lot more you can do with Facebook for Websites. To see for yourself, visit developers.facebook.com, then click **Add Facebook to my site**.

> **FRIEND-LY ADVICE**
>
> Implementing Facebook for Websites on your website isn't for amateur website builders. In many cases, it requires tapping in to Facebook's API (application programming interface), which is best left to skilled and creative website developers, engineers, and programmers.

Tapping the Power of Places and Deals

And don't forget about using Facebook Places and Facebook Deals to connect with customers when they're out and about. Facebook Places enables you to establish a business presence on Facebook, so members can search for and locate your business when in need of the products and services you offer. You can also create Check-in Deals and run them across multiple store locations. When members check in to your Facebook Place, they see the offer and can click to take advantage of it.

For more about using Facebook Places and Deals in your business, check out Chapter 19.

Establishing a Following with Groups

Another option that businesses, brands, and organizations have for connecting and engaging with Facebook members is to create a Facebook Group. While groups have a similar look and feel to Pages, Facebook intends for them to serve different purposes. While Pages are managed by businesses or brands, groups are managed by Facebook members and are great for connecting with high school classmates, organizing family members for a reunion or Mom's surprise 75th birthday party, generating discussion among book club members, and so on.

While individuals—rather than businesses—tend to start and manage Facebook Groups, that doesn't mean you can't use them for business purposes. Because you can set groups as private/for members only, creating a group and inviting select business customers and brand advocates to join and engage with one another is a great way to facilitate focus groups and gain valuable insight into customer wants and needs.

Similarly, you can join groups that focus on topics related to your business or brand—assuming they're open to all Facebook members—and listen in to what people are saying. If appropriate to the situation, you can even respond officially as a company representative.

For more information on Facebook Groups, check out Chapter 9, where we show you how to join a group, form groups of your own, engage in group discussions, and share stuff with fellow group members.

Engaging Members with Facebook Applications

Suppose you want your customers to be able to use your company website to share video testimonials about your business, photos of themselves using your products or services, or daily updates of their related activities. You'd spend a fortune designing, programming, and engineering your site to handle the activity and resulting traffic. Facebook handles all of that for you, and it doesn't cost you a cent.

Facebook's core applications—which include status updates, photos, and video—are all available for you to use for business purposes. Want to hold a promotion to see who can create the best video featuring your products or services? With Facebook's video application, your customers can upload user-generated video files to Facebook and post them to your Page's Wall, and you can call attention to them through status updates and notes.

With a little creativity, you're sure to figure out how your business can leverage Facebook's applications for business purposes. Let's say you run a chain of florist shops and you want your customers on Facebook to be able to send their Facebook friends virtual flower arrangements. As members send virtual flowers back and forth on Facebook, you gain valuable visibility among people most inclined to send real flowers later on.

Great idea! But because Facebook doesn't have a suitable application of its own, you'd have to build a virtual flower application in line with Facebook's standards and guidelines for applications. Sound complicated? It is, which is why you should work with a professional Facebook application developer—someone who's successfully built Facebook apps before and knows her way around Facebook's development landscape.

For a list of developers who can help your business build the Facebook application of your dreams, visit developers.facebook.com/preferreddevelopers. There, you'll find a list of experienced and trusted developers who are included in Facebook's Preferred Developer Consultant Program.

Do's and Don'ts of Doing Business on Facebook

If you're not careful, social-media marketing, particularly on Facebook, can do more harm than good. Attempting to go viral goes both ways: say the right thing, and the good word can spread like wildfire; say the wrong thing, and you'll be engulfed by that wildfire. To improve your odds of success, adhere to the following do's and don'ts of marketing on Facebook:

- **Do engage with your fans.** When a fan leaves a comment on one of your status updates, thank her, answer her question, or comment back (if appropriate). If a fan posts a photo or video on your Wall, make a comment or click the **Like** button if, indeed, you appreciate the post.

- **Do be authentic and transparent.** We live in the age of reality, where everyone feels they're entitled to know everyone else's business. (You can thank reality TV and cable news for that.) On Facebook, the same holds true for your business. If you launch a Facebook Page, fans expect you to be real, and that means transparent and authentic. No hidden agendas allowed.

- **Don't self-promote too much.** Remember, it's called social networking, not social selling. While your customers expect you to be on Facebook, they don't want you constantly accosting them with sales pitches.

- **Do choose a great Profile image.** Make sure it accurately and appropriately shows who or what you are. For most businesses, this means posting the company logo or an image of its brand-defining product or service.

- **Don't use "I" statements in status updates or notes.** A business is not an "I," it's a "We." If you post a status update about exhibiting at a conference or trade show, you wouldn't say, "I am exhibiting at such-and-such show later this week. Stop by and see me in booth number 513." Rather, you'd write something like, "XYZ Products will be exhibiting at such-and-such show later this week. Stop by and see us in booth number 513."

- **Do flesh out your Profile.** Be complete, and include everything you're asked to provide in your Profile. Don't leave your fans—your customers and prospects—hanging. Give them all the information they need.

- **Don't create multiple Pages for multiple products.** You may not have the resources to keep all the Pages up-to-date and relevant, not to mention that you'll dilute your brand.

- **Do create and post notes.** Like entries on company blogs, Facebook Notes have the potential to be indexed by search engines, which means your notes—if packed with great keywords and phrases, and relevant to your customers and branding goals—can help attract more fans and traffic.

- **Do choose a vanity URL.** Facebook allows Page owners to request a specific URL for each of their Pages. So rather than live with the Facebook-generated URL, which usually contains a series of numbers and symbols that are difficult to remember, you can tell customers to find you on Facebook at www.facebook.com/yourcompanyname. (To obtain a vanity URL, your Page must have a certain number of fans, and Facebook must approve your request. More about this in Chapter 17.)

- **Don't go long stretches without posting a status update.** Fans and passersby have a reasonable expectation that your Facebook Page is going to be kept up-to-date, and the number one way of doing that is to create and post a consistent stream of status updates. One update per day is ideal, but if you can't do that, one every other day should suffice.

- **Don't put all your eggs in one Facebook basket.** Facebook is not the be-all, end-all marketing vehicle. It's just one more weapon in your marketing arsenal.

- **Don't forget everything you already know about marketing.** Facebook is just like every other marketing channel—you have to know your audience and what's considered the most acceptable way of engaging with that audience in that particular channel.

- **Do measure your efforts.** ROI on Facebook comes by way of ROE (return on engagement). Areas to measure include website traffic from Facebook, search engine results and ranking, inbound links to your website, number of fans or group members, comments on status updates, and mentions of your brand as a result of your Facebook-related activity.

The Least You Need to Know

- The business case for Facebook? 620,000,000+ people happily gathered in one central location online, many of whom are your customers and expect to see your business or brand there.

- At the very least, your business should have its own Page to function as its base of operations on Facebook.

- Cross-promote your Facebook Page and company website to drive traffic to each.

- Facebook ads give you the power to target Facebook users by locale and demographic.

- Use the Groups feature and business apps to further engage customers and prospects on Facebook.

Launching and Managing a Business Page

In This Chapter

- Grasping the marketing potential of a Page
- Building and customizing a Page
- Keeping your Page fresh with relevant, compelling content
- Attracting traffic
- Tracking results with Page Insights (analytics)

As a business or organization, you can establish a presence on Facebook by creating and customizing your very own Pages. A Page is a public Profile that enables you to share your business or organization and any products or services you offer with Facebook members.

Your Page can function as the central location for your business on Facebook, or you can use Pages to highlight very specific products or services—using them as you might use landing pages on the web. Through your Pages, you can post status updates to keep current and prospective customers informed and up-to-date. If your business or organization has a blog, you can even set up a feed on your Page that automatically pulls blog posts onto the Page.

Build a quality Page, populate it with relevant and compelling content, and begin to attract fans. When fans interact with your Page, these interactions can appear in their News Feeds, where their friends can find out about your Page and business and help spread the word. Do it right, and you may be able to spark a word-of-mouth promotional wildfire that advertises for you! In this chapter, we show you how.

The Business Case for a Page

In Facebook's early childhood, the entrance fee for establishing a business presence on Facebook excluded all but the richest corporations. Now any company or organization can launch a Facebook Page for free in a matter of minutes and use the Page as a launch pad for an effective social-media marketing campaign.

In Chapter 16, we make a case for doing business on Facebook. The same rationale applies to creating a Facebook Page. In fact, if you've decided to do business on Facebook, creating a Page for your business and/or the products and services you're selling is a no-brainer. Pages are free, they provide a base of operations, and they enable you to take the lead in discussions revolving around your business or organization and any products or services you offer.

> **POKE**
>
> Organizations, products, or services that have a strong brand presence often find that they're already on Facebook. Facebook members may create their own Facebook Groups or Pages where they discuss an organization's merits (or shortcomings) or discuss its products or services. This can be very positive for your organization, but you should still launch an official Page of your own so you can play a leadership role in any associated communities. You can then invite members of the other communities, who have already expressed an interest in your offerings, to become fans of your Page by liking it.

Crafting and Customizing Your Page

Your Page is your business's or organization's face on Facebook, so you want it to create a good and lasting first impression. You want people who see it to like it and become fans so you can communicate with them directly. In the following sections, we show you how to lay the groundwork for a quality Page and then step you through the process of creating it.

Laying the Groundwork

Just because Facebook Pages are free to create doesn't mean they should look cheap. You should invest at least as much time preparing to create a Page as you would spend on creating a quality advertisement for your organization. Prior to creating a Page, make sure the following pieces are in place:

- **Purpose:** A Page without a purpose usually lacks impact.

- **Page name:** Settle on a name for your Page that customers and prospects are likely to recognize. You can't change the Page name after 100 people like it, so pick the right name the first time. Remember, you're trying to create brand identity, so consistency is key—the name should match whatever name you use offline.

- **Quality images:** Strictly speaking, images are optional, but if you want to appeal to the masses, you'd better use a high-quality image (something that puts a face on your business or organization) for your Profile picture. Consider using your organization's logo or a photo of the primary product you're showcasing.

- **Content:** Content is key in turning fans into customers and customers into fans.

Generally speaking, the main goal of your Page should be to convince visitors to become fans by clicking the **Like** button and regularly engaging with your business or organization on Facebook. You may also have a secondary goal, such as encouraging Facebook members to visit your organization's website, keep fans in the loop concerning newsworthy events, gather insight into customer wants and needs, or inform fans of special deals and offers on your products and services. Your ultimate goal may be to sell, but when it comes to Facebook, selling shouldn't be the purpose; instead, you should use it to warm up prospects and customers, create community, and build trust.

If your company manufactures aftermarket parts for motorcycles, you may want to post announcements of upcoming races or rallies, videos showing how to install products, and photos of your parts on cool-looking bikes. If you're a restaurant, posting your menu, phone number, address, and a map of your location may be a good idea. Or you might want to post a much sought-after recipe that you're comfortable sharing with the public or a link to a great review in a local magazine or on a website. If you're promoting a film, you'll want to include a trailer and create an event promoting the movie's premier. If you run a bed and breakfast in southern Vermont, you'll want to post ski conditions for the local resort, notices of availability, and specials on rooms in the off-season. Whatever you want to include, have it ready when you begin creating your Page. You'll find more details on populating your Page with relevant and compelling content later in this chapter.

Focus your efforts on serving the community rather than your own interests. Posting your entire product catalog is probably a bad idea, because it sends a clear message that you're only interested in selling products and collecting money. Instead, consider posting a tip on how customers can enhance their experience with a particular product.

POKE

Remember, it's called *social networking,* not *social selling.* While 90 percent of Facebook members expect businesses and organizations to have a presence on Facebook and other social-networking platforms and services, only 25 percent want to be marketed to. Facebook members prefer evangelizing brands themselves over being sold to.

Creating Your Page

The process of creating a Page is relatively easy. You click a link, enter your preferences and content via a series of forms, and your Page is up and running. The following list leads you through the process step by step:

1. Scroll to the bottom of the Facebook screen you're on (down to the footer) and click **Create a Page**. Six options appear.

2. Do one of the following depending on the type of Page you're creating:

- Click **Local Business or Place**, select the category that best describes your business, and fill in the requested information.

- Click **Company, Organization, or Institution** and then select the category that most closely represents the company, organization, or institution you want to promote.

- Click **Brand or Product** and then select the category that most closely represents the brand or product you're going to promote.

- Click **Artist, Band or Public Figure** and select the category for the artist, band, or public figure you want to promote.

- Click **Entertainment** and choose the category of the entity you want to promote.

- Click **Cause or Community** and type in the name of the cause or community you want to promote.

3. Click the checkbox next to "I agree to Facebook Pages Terms."

4. Click **Get Started**. Facebook creates and displays your Page and presents six steps to getting started.

5. Click **Upload an Image from Your Computer** (in the first area), and then upload the image you want to use to represent this Page. (For more about uploading photos and other images, see Chapter 7.)

6. Click **Edit Info** under your Page name, and on the next screen—the **Basic Information** tab of the administrative area of the Page—write a short description about the Page in the **About** field, followed by a brief but detailed description of whatever the Page is about in the **Description** box, and your website address in the **Website** field. Depending what type of Page you're creating, you may have more areas to fill in, which you can do now or later. When you're done, click **Save Changes**.

7. Post status updates or other content at least three times a week to attract fans and keep them engaged. You can post status updates to the Page's Wall, or post photos, videos, events, and notes on separate tabs. More details on populating your Page with relevant and compelling content are provided later in this chapter.

Change the image

Write a blurb

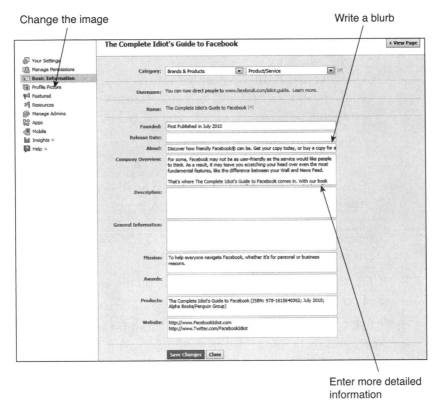

Enter more detailed information

Flesh out your Page with an image and text.

Getting Back to Your Page

After creating your Page, you can always return to the administrative area to make changes. Regardless of what you're doing in Facebook, click on **Home** (in the top menu), then **Pages** or the name of the Page (in the left menu). What happens next varies depending on the number of Pages you have:

- If you have only one Page, the public view of the Page shows up. Click the **Edit Page** link (at the top of the right column) to display the administrative area of the Page on a screen where you can edit its content and settings.

- If you have two or more Pages, they appear in a list. Click the title of the Page you want to edit, followed by the **Edit Page** link at the top of the right column to display the administrative area of the Page on a screen where you can edit its content and settings.

Adjusting Your Page Settings

Immediately after creating your Page, check its settings and adjust them if necessary to control how your Page operates and shares information. To pull up your Page settings, head to the Page and then click **Edit Page** (at the top of the right column).

To edit any of the settings or access any of the administrative areas of the Page, click the appropriate link in the left menu. You can adjust the following items:

- **Your Settings:** Here, you can set preferences for how your posts to your Page appear and whether you'd like to receive e-mail notifications when people post or comment on your Page. We recommend keeping the default setting for both items. When posting to your Page, you should always do so as the Page because there's no "I" when communicating on behalf of a business or brand. Leaving **Posting Preferences** checked ensures all your posts will be displayed as coming from the same name associated with the Page, not the name associated with your personal Facebook account. **Email Notifications** are important because they keep you informed whenever someone posts to your Page.

You can change Posting Preferences and Email Notifications for your Page.

- **Manage Permissions:** These options enable you to limit
  access to your Page to only the countries you specify, set a
  minimum age for accessing the Page, or change the Page's
  visibility status. Also, and this is very important, since
  Facebook's default setting for the Page's visibility is publicly
  visible, consider changing it to "Only admins can see this
  page" until you are ready for the world to see your new creation. Other options here allow you to control access to the
  Page's Wall. You can specify whether you want only the Page
  to be able to post to the Wall or the Page and its users, choose
  which tab first appears whenever a visitor or fan lands on the
  Page, control whether comments on posts are expanded by
  default, and limit what users can post on the Page.

- **Basic Information:** Depending on the type of Page you
  have, here you're able to add and edit the basic information
  about your business, organization, brand, or cause, including
  biographical data and website address.

- **Profile Picture:** This is where you add, edit, or delete your
  Profile picture. You can either browse for an image on your
  computer to upload or take a picture of yourself if you per-
  sonally are the subject of the Page. You can even edit your
  thumbnail image.

- **Featured:** These settings pertain to featuring other Pages
  and your own Page's admins on the Page. When you use
  Facebook As Page (as opposed to using your personal

Facebook account to navigate the site), your Page has the opportunity to like other Pages. Once your Page likes another Page, the liked Page is displayed on the left side of your Page. The **Add Featured Likes** setting allows you to identify which of the Pages your Page likes show up on your Wall. The **Add Featured Page Owners** setting allows you to publicly display your Page's Admins on your Page.

- **Resources:** Here you find links to areas of Facebook that are helpful when attempting to further optimize your Page, connect with other members, and more.

- **Admins:** Here you control who, besides you, can administer the Page. Because most businesses and organizations have more than one person capable of managing their Page, Facebook allows you to assign an unlimited number of admins. Admins, who access your Page through their personal accounts, by default remain anonymous to your Page's users and can have their privileges revoked at any time by the Page's creator.

- **Applications:** As we covered in Chapter 13, your Facebook account comes preloaded with apps, and the same is true for a Facebook Page. Here, you can adjust settings for Photos, Links, Events, Notes, Videos, and any other apps you add, or you can delete them altogether. For example, you can use the Links settings to specify whether fans can post links to the Page or only allow admins to do so.

- **Mobile:** Mobile enables you to sign up to receive text messages from Facebook notifying you of activity on your Page. See Chapter 15 for more about Facebook Mobile.

- **Insights:** If you want to learn about the people who like your Page and how they interact with your content, click the **Insights** tab. Here, you'll find all sorts of stats and data, including the number of active users broken down by day, week, and month; number of post views and items commented on; user demographics, including age, gender, and geographical location; and more.

Hiding or Deleting Pages

By default, your Page is visible to everyone on Facebook. If it's currently under construction, you may want to hide it. To hide your Page, head to the Page and click **Edit Page** (at the top of the right column). Click **Manage Permissions**, click the **Page Visibility** checkbox next to **Only admins can see this page**, and click **Save Changes**.

Assuming a Page has outlived its usefulness, you can delete it for good. Click **Edit Page**, click the **Manage Permissions** tab, and, at the bottom of the Page, click the **Permanently delete** link. When the confirmation dialog box pops up, click **Delete**.

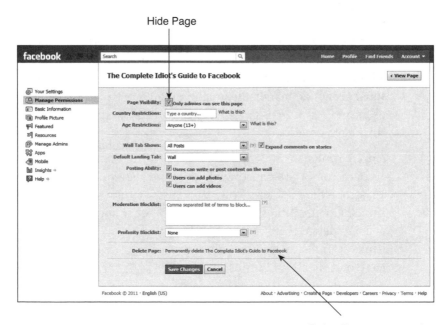

You can hide or delete your Page.

Adding Compelling Content to Your Page

Your Page is very similar to your personal Profile, complete with multiple tabs for posting status updates to the Wall, uploading photos, and hosting discussions. Use your Page accordingly to engage fans, keep them coming back for more, and inspire them to share your Page with their friends.

Engage is the keyword here. This Page isn't as much about you, your business, or your products as it is about the topics your fans are interested in. We're not saying you should pander to the masses—that could turn fans off, too. You want to size up your audience and deliver the content they crave in a way that meets or exceeds their expectations. If you're in the restaurant biz, that may mean posting this week's specials. If you're promoting your band, it might mean posting lyrics or updates about the current tour. If you manufacture 120 different styles of motorcycle seats, you may end up fielding lots of customer service questions about motorcycle seat fitment. Treat your fans like friends instead of customers or clients, and you're likely to hit the bull's-eye, unless of course your customers are using your Page for customer service–related questions.

Use your Page to engage fans the same way you use your Profile to engage friends.

WHOA!

Resist the urge to post your product catalog. Far too many businesses treat social media, which is intended to be dynamic and interactive, as a shell for static web content. They essentially copy web content and post it on Facebook. This is ineffective and likely to do more harm than good.

Expanding Content with Other Facebook Apps

In addition to posting status updates and photos and facilitating discussions, consider using other Facebook applications to engage the people who like your Page. You can use the Events app to announce special occasions, such as a grand opening, a conference, or a trade show. You can post a note to focus the spotlight on your "Fan of the Month" or announce the results of a recent promotion. Use your imagination to think up clever uses for Facebook's standard apps.

Accessorizing Your Page with Third-Party Apps

To further enhance your Page, you can add business apps from third-party developers. Following are some examples:

- **Promotions** for Pages enable you to run branded, interactive promotions on your Pages, including sweepstakes, contests, coupon giveaways, instant wins, gifting, and quizzes.

- **Testimonials** and **Reviews** enable you to collect customer testimonials and product/service reviews from Facebook fans and display them on your Page.

- **Eventbrite** provides tools for bringing people together for an event and selling tickets. If you're a budding rock star, this app could come in very handy.

- **Polls** make it easy to create online polls and analyze results with graphs that illustrate user responses across multiple demographics.

Feeding Your Blog to Your Facebook Business Page

If you already maintain a blog outside Facebook, don't waste time manually posting content to your blog and then reposting it on Facebook. You can set up a feed on your Page that automatically pulls entries from your blog and displays them on your Facebook Page as notes. To set up an incoming blog feed, here's what you do:

1. Display the Page on which you want the feed to appear.

2. Click **Edit Page** (in the top right corner of the Page). The Page settings appear.

3. Click **Apps** in the left column.

4. Under Notes, click **Edit Settings**. The Edit Notes Settings dialog box appears.

5. On the Tab line, click **add** next to Available, and then click **Okay**. (If **remove** appears next to Added, click **Okay** and proceed to step 6.) This adds a Notes tab to your Page and you're now ready to import notes.

6. Click **Go to App** (below Notes).

7. Click **Edit import settings** (at the bottom of the left column, under Subscribe).

8. Click in the **Enter a website or RSS/Atom feed address** box and type the address of your blog or RSS or Atom feed.

9. Click the checkbox next to **By entering a URL ....**

10. Click **Start Importing**. Assuming everything works according to plan, Facebook displays a preview of the imported blog.

11. Check the preview, and if it looks right, click **Confirm** (at the top of the Page). If it doesn't look right, or you just decide not to move forward with the import, click **Cancel**.

Set up a blog feed to pull posts from an existing blog and display them as notes.

Building and Maintaining Your Fan Base

"If you build it, they will come," is as untrue a statement on Facebook as it is throughout the rest of the web. Building, growing, and maintaining an active community of fans through a Facebook Page requires the following two key components:

- **A killer Page** with fresh, engaging, and interactive content.

- **Promotion.** Yep, that's right. You build a Page to promote something, and then you have to promote your Page. It never stops.

Facebook can't help you with the first component. It's entirely up to you to keep the content on your Page fresh and compelling and interact with fans regularly and in a meaningful way. Facebook does, however, provide you with several tools for promoting your Page:

- **Become your own number one fan.** Pull up your Page and click the **Like** button (to the right of the Page title). Now at least your Page has one fan. When you become a fan, all your friends are notified via their News Feeds.

- **Invite your friends.** Click **Suggest to Friends** (in the right column of the Page) and Facebook sends a message to the friends you think will be interested in the Page.

- **Send updates to fans.** If you have something to offer that's really good, you can send an update to fans by clicking **Edit Page** (at the top of the right column) followed by **Resources** in the left column, and **Send an Update** under **Connect with people**.

- **Link your Page to Twitter.** Twitter is a very popular microblogging platform. If you don't have a Twitter account yet, register for one at twitter.com and then edit your Page to link it to Twitter. This option is available by visiting www.facebook.com/twitter.

- **Place a Like button or Like box on your website or blog.** Facebook's Like button lets the people who visit your website or blog share pages from your site back to their Facebook Profile with a single click. The Like box allows your website or blog visitors to like your Facebook Page and view its most recent stream of activity directly from your site. To gain access to the code necessary to make these and other "social plugins" work on your website or blog, click **Edit Page** (in the top right column of your Page), and click **Resources** in the left column followed by the **Use social plugins** link (under Connect with people). Follow the instructions on the resulting screen to access the code you need.

- **Give your Page its own vanity URL.** As soon as your Page has a certain number of fans (Facebook set the minimum at 25 last we checked), you can claim a vanity URL for your Page—a web address that more clearly and simply reflects the Page title. Go to www.facebook.com/username, click **Set a user name** for your Pages (below the box that allows you to set a username for your Profile), and follow the on-screen instructions.

POKE

Facebook is very particular about the way you promote your Page. Click the **Best Practice for Marketing on Facebook** link inside the **Resources** area of your Page's settings for additional guidance on promoting your Facebook Page outside Facebook.

Tracking Page Effectiveness with Page Insights

Wondering how many people visit your Page every day? Want to know the number and demographics of your Facebook fans and how frequently fans interact with your Page? Then pull up your Page Insights (Facebook's term for analytics). From your Page, click **View Insights** (right menu). Here you'll find vital metrics related to your Page's performance, including daily, weekly, and monthly active users; unique Page views; gender and age of your visitors; countries, cities, and languages of your visitors; and more.

To get the most out of your business activities on Facebook, you need to know what's working and what's not, which content your fans interact with most, and how fans interact with your brand and with one another. While you can glean some of this information from scanning each individual item on your Page's Wall, doing so is tedious and prone to miscalculation.

Page Insights present valuable statistics related to your Page.

Enter Page Insights. From posting quality scores that measure how engaging your posts have been over a rolling seven-day period, to the number of fans interacting with your content and the number of interactions per post, Facebook provides the information you need to quickly evaluate the effectiveness of your efforts and your return on investment (ROI).

Facebook also e-mails you a weekly summary of your Insights, informing you of the number of fans you've gained (or lost) during the week; the number of Wall posts, comments, and likes; and the number of visits to the Page. The message includes links to various Facebook features that can help you build your user base.

The Least You Need to Know

- Businesses, organizations, and individuals interested in leveraging the power of online community should have a Facebook Page.

- This is social networking. It's not social selling. Use your Page to interact with customers and brand advocates as you would interact with colleagues and Facebook friends.

- To do anything related to Pages, click **Home**, and click **Pages** or the name of your Page in the left column.

- Use all the tools in the shed to build your Page, including status updates, photos, notes, events, links, videos, discussions, and third-party apps.

- To build, maintain, and grow a fan base, keep your Page updated with clever, relevant content and promote the heck out of your Page.

- Cross-promote your Page and your website or blog by linking to your site from your Page and from your Page to your website or blog.

- Use Page Insights to measure and monitor traffic, evaluate ROI, and identify obstacles to engagement.

Mastering the Soft Sell with Social Ads

In This Chapter

- Recognizing the potential of Facebook ads
- Using Facebook ads strategically in your marketing campaigns
- Doing the essential prep work
- Following Facebook's rules and regulations for posting ads
- Creating a Facebook ad that achieves your goals

Posting advertisements for your business on Facebook via personal status updates is like announcing a 75 percent off sale during the singing of "The Star-Spangled Banner." It'll earn you more enemies than friends. You can get away with it on a business Page, as explained in Chapter 17, but don't do it from your personal Facebook account. If you want to advertise, you need to carefully craft and post ads using Facebook Ads, the site's official advertising platform.

In this chapter, we introduce you to the potential benefits (and a few drawbacks) of Facebook advertising, step you through the process of developing an effective strategy, show you how to prepare your ads, and then assist you in launching and managing your advertising campaign.

Weighing the Pros and Cons of Facebook Ads

You can receive a great deal of word-of-mouth advertising on Facebook without spending a penny, so you may be wondering whether paid advertising is worth it. We can't answer that question for you, but we can provide you with the pros and cons to consider in making this decision for yourself.

Potential Benefits

When deciding where to invest your advertising budget, consider the following benefits of Facebook ads:

- **More than 620 million active members:** A lot of people spend a lot of time on Facebook—even more time than they spend watching TV, glancing at billboards, reading newspapers or magazines, or browsing the web. In other words, they're more likely to see an ad on Facebook than anywhere else.

- **Ability to target a specific demographic and locale:** Facebook enables you to target your ads by age, gender, education, geography, marital status, and more, so you stand to get more bang for your buck than with more generalized CPC (cost-per-click) advertising on the web. In addition, Facebook members are more motivated to provide accurate information about themselves and keep it up-to-date, meaning your ads are more likely to be viewed by people who are who they say they are.

- **Ability to target keywords:** You can pack your ad with keywords to place your ad in front of Facebook members who express an interest in your products or services.

- **Potential bump from social interaction:** Your ad can include a call to action to do something on Facebook, such as become a fan or join a group. Whenever someone performs that call to action, it's likely to be posted to his Wall and News Feed where his friends can see it. This provides extra mileage for your ad.

- **Affordability and scalability:** You can spend as much or as little money per day as you like on your Facebook ads. Facebook charges by cost per click (CPC) or cost per thousand impressions (CPM; the M stands for the "milli" in the metric system, not "millions"). *Impression* means that the ad appears on a member's screen when they're using Facebook, regardless of whether a user clicks it or even sees it.

- **Ability to measure your ad's performance:** Facebook provides basic analytics so you can check your account for each ad's clicks, impressions, CPC, and CPM.

Potential Drawbacks

Facebook ads may seem like the ideal solution for businesses or organizations of any size, but they're not without some potential drawbacks, including the following:

- **Lack of interest in ads:** People on Facebook gather to connect and chat, not shop. Your ads are more like billboards or magazine advertisements that people may glance at in the midst of doing something else.

- **Poor timing versus search engine marketing:** When web users search on Google, Yahoo!, Bing, or other search engines, they're often trying to find a solution, product, or service. With search engine marketing, your ad catches them at the right time. This doesn't occur on Facebook and other social-media sites.

- **Lack of trust:** Facebook isn't very selective in determining who can advertise. As a result, many ads promote questionable products or services that turn off Facebook users to *all* ads.

Laying the Groundwork

You can slap together a Facebook ad in minutes, but before launching your first advertising campaign, spend some time brushing up on Facebook's rules and regulations, developing a strategy, and preparing the components of your ad—your message and graphic.

Brushing Up on Facebook Ads Rules and Regulations

To remain in good standing with Facebook, follow its rules. For an exhaustive (and exhausting) list of rules, head to www.facebook.com/ad_guidelines.php. The following list highlights the major do's and don'ts:

- No multiple accounts or automated creation of accounts for advertising purposes.

- No funny business on landing pages your ads link to, including pop-overs, pop-unders, fake close buttons, or bait-and-switch URLs (a link that makes visitors think they're going to a particular place but end up somewhere else).

- No using the Facebook name, brand, or logos in a way that even hints that Facebook endorses you, your company, or your products.

- No false, fraudulent, or deceptive ads.

- No lewd, crude, or otherwise inappropriate language or obscene, libelous, harassing, insulting, or unlawful content, including hate speech.

- No advertising firearms, illicit drugs, scams, get-rich-quick schemes, adult "friend finders," uncertified pharmaceutical products, nonaccredited colleges, or other goods or services that could be deemed dangerous, illegal, or of questionable value.

- Adhere to all of Facebook's privacy guidelines regarding member content.

- No spamming.

- Ads for alcoholic beverages or adult-related products or services must be age appropriate and not designed to lure minors, and ads for gambling-related services, including any online casinos, sports books, bingo, or poker, may not be posted without authorization from Facebook.

- No copyright infringement.

- No using ads to trick users into downloading spyware or malware.

Setting a Measurable Goal

To determine how well an advertising campaign is performing, start with a measurable goal. With a Facebook ad, you typically want to set two measurable goals: one relating to traffic and the other to conversion rates. Specify how much traffic or what percentage increase in traffic from Facebook to your landing page or website you expect your ad campaign to generate. For conversion rates, specify the percentage of people who arrived from Facebook and then succeeded in performing the call to action included in the ad.

The goals you set are entirely up to you. You can set goals according to the number of visitors, percentage increase in visitors, CPC, or some other benchmark.

After setting one or more measurable goals, make sure you have the analytics in place to track each ad's success. Facebook can provide you with some statistics that apply directly to your ad, such as number of impressions or number of times an ad was clicked. To measure click-through or conversion rates, however, you must have analytics installed on your website or landing page. Google Analytics (www. google.com/analytics) is an excellent choice, and it's free!

The goal you set influences your strategy and the type of advertising you choose to do on Facebook:

- **Pay-per-click advertising:** When you're paying per click, targeting ads to the most appropriate demographic and geographical area is of prime importance. In addition, make sure your ad and landing page (a Facebook Page or a page on your website) are well coordinated to encourage and facilitate your call to action.

- **Pay-per-view advertising:** When you're paying for impressions, brand identity is most important. The graphic you use should clearly communicate your brand or company, and the text should be clear and informative.

Targeting a Demographic and Locale

Make the most of the targeting features in Facebook ads. If you're running a local pizzeria, advertising to the entire country is probably a bad idea—especially if you're offering free delivery. You'll get more bang for your advertising buck by targeting a specific location. Likewise, if whatever you're advertising is more likely to appeal to a certain age group or gender, specify your target demographic when creating your ad.

Listing a Few Keywords

In search engine optimization (SEO), web marketers use meta data such as page titles, page descriptions, and keywords to attract search engine attention and improve page rankings in search results. Keywords can play a similar role in Facebook ads—enabling Facebook to target specific ads to Facebook users who express an interest in a certain topic (by mentioning it in their Profiles, Wall posts, notes, and even in their status updates).

Prior to creating an ad, invest some thought in which words and phrases Facebook members are likely to use in describing the product or service you're advertising. Sprinkle these keywords and phrases generously throughout your ad.

Settling on a Call to Action

Every ad, especially the pay-per-click variety, should include a call to action—a clear, direct message telling whoever is looking at the ad what to do. You usually want people to do two things: first, click on your ad, and then do something when they reach your website or landing page, such as register, order, shop, buy, obtain a quote, or check out special offers. These two goals should be well-coordinated;

if your ad sets certain expectations, your website must meet or exceed those expectations and facilitate the visitor's ability to follow through on your call to action.

A call to action may also apply to activity within Facebook, such as becoming a fan, joining a brand-based group, or registering for an event.

Composing an Effective Message

In a Facebook ad, you don't have a lot of room to elaborate. You pretty much have to make your point in 25 words or fewer (25 characters for the title and 135 characters for the body). Use these words efficiently by composing a concise message that speaks clearly and directly to your audience. Here are some tips for creating quality ad copy:

- Be direct.
- Be clear.
- Keep it simple. Save the details for your website or landing page.
- Focus on the call to action.
- To reinforce brand identity, use your company or product name in the ad title or the body of the ad.
- Proofread the ad carefully before posting it. Nothing drives customers away more quickly than poor grammar and typos.

Finding Just the Right Picture

A high-quality image can catch the eye and reinforce the message your ad conveys. When selecting an image, make sure it's attractive and relevant to the product or service you're advertising.

The maximum image size is 80 pixels tall by 110 pixels wide, which is pretty small. If your image contains text, don't expect it to be readable. The image should have an aspect ratio (height:width) of 4:3 or 16:9. Facebook resizes the image for you, if necessary, but for best quality, size it yourself before uploading it. No animated graphics or flash images are allowed.

Prior to posting a photo or image, open it in a photo-editing or graphics program and play around with the brightness, contrast, and color balance to achieve the highest quality possible. Photos in particular often appear too dark when displayed on a computer screen. (For more about image quality, see Chapter 7.)

Launching Your Advertising Campaign

After laying the groundwork, launching your ad campaign is a snap. All you need to do is transfer your text, upload an image, specify your targeted demographic, and choose a plan and pricing. The following sections step you through the process.

Creating Your Ad

To get started, scroll to the bottom of any Facebook Page, click **Advertising**, and click **Create an Ad** (upper right). The Advertise on Facebook screen appears requesting the following four items:

- **Destination:** You have two options here. To link to a website or landing page outside Facebook, select **External URL** from the drop-down menu and type the page's web address (URL) in the URL box that appears below the menu. If you have a Page, app, Event, or Place on Facebook that you want to link to, select the item from the drop-down list. (This option is available only if you have a Page, Group, or Event on Facebook.)

- **Title:** Type your ad title (up to 25 characters). If you're linking to something on Facebook, the title you already gave your Page, Group, app, or Event appears in this box, and you're unable to edit it, which is good—you want it to be consistent.

- **Body:** Type the ad copy (up to 135 characters), being sure to include a clear call to action.

- **Image:** Click **Choose File** and follow the on-screen cues to select and upload an image stored on your computer.

After entering all four items, click the **Continue** button. The Targeting options appear. You may need to scroll down to see them.

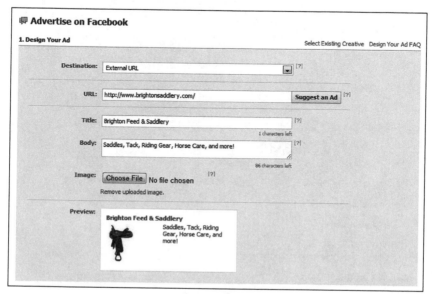

Create your Facebook ad.

Targeting Your Demographic

By default, Facebook targets your ad to a very broad demographic—Facebook members 18 years and older who live in the default location (for example, the United States). Facebook enables you to narrow your focus by location, age, gender, likes and interests, education, workplace, relationships, connections, and so on. Simply enter your preferences. As you change settings, Facebook displays (on the right side of the screen) an estimate of the number of members that fit the targeted demographic.

When you're done, click the **Continue** button. The Campaigns and Pricing options appear.

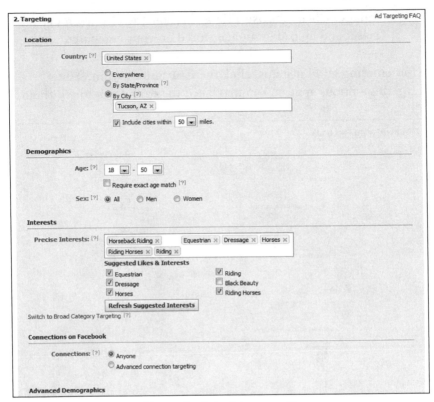

Target the desired demographic.

Choosing a Campaign, Pricing, and Scheduling

After creating and targeting your ad, you must set up your ad campaign by entering your preferences for the following categories:

- **Campaign & Budget:** You can type a name for a new or existing campaign. Multiple ads in the same campaign share a daily budget and schedule. The budget is the total amount you want to spend per day or over the lifetime of the campaign. The minimum is $1.

- **Schedule:** You can choose to have your ad run continuously starting today or between two specified dates and times.

- **Pricing:** Here, you choose between Pay for Impressions or Pay for Clicks. Facebook suggests a bid amount, which you can raise or lower depending on the number of clicks or impressions you want to buy. (How much you're willing to bid affects ad placement, which generally affects the performance of the ad.)

Enter preferences for your ad campaign.

After entering your preferences, click the **Review Ad** button. The Review Ad page appears, displaying your ad and details about your campaign.

Reviewing and Approving Your Ad

The Review Ad page shows you how your ad will appear in Facebook, provides details about the ad campaign, and prompts you to enter payment information. Carefully examine your ad and all details about it. You can make changes by clicking the **Edit Ad** link.

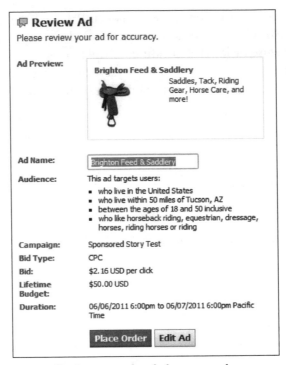

Review your ad and place your order.

Monitoring and Fine-Tuning Your Campaign

Your ad campaign is up and running. Now you can kick back, cross your fingers, and hope it meets your goals, right? Not quite. You should keep tabs on your campaign and be prepared to make adjustments.

After a day or two, check your ad's click-through rate, along with its total clicks, impressions, and average CPC or CPM. To view these statistics, click **Advertising** (at the bottom of any Facebook Page) and then the name of the campaign on the following screen. From this page, you can click ad attributes to change them.

If your ad is not quite meeting your expectations, consider making any of the following adjustments:

- Try a different call to action if Facebook members are not responding to your ad.

- Adjust your targeting preferences to be more restrictive if your conversion rate is low, meaning that your ad is getting plenty of impressions or clicks but they aren't translating into the desired activity.

- Adjust your targeting preferences to be less restrictive if your ad's impressions or clicks are too low.

- Try simplifying your ad.

- Try a different image.

The Least You Need to Know

- Use ads as a component of your relationship-marketing efforts on Facebook. Don't expect them to generate direct sales.

- Prior to creating an ad, set a clear goal so you can measure its success.

- Prepare your ad copy and image prior to creating an ad, so you're not just slapping something together at the last minute.

- To create an ad, click **Advertising** (at the bottom of any Facebook Page), click **Create an Ad**, and follow the on-screen instructions.

- You can monitor and make changes to ads at any time. Click **Advertising** and then click the name of the campaign on the following screen.

Marketing with Places and Deals

In This Chapter

- Claiming and customizing your Facebook Place
- Merging your Place with your Page
- Offering Check-in Deals without the hassles of coupons
- Spreading the word about your Place and Check-in Deals

Facebook features two tools that businesses can use to tap the power of location marketing: Facebook Places and Check-in Deals. Location marketing consists of presenting content to customers and prospects that's relevant to their current location. For example, if you're managing a clothing store and need to clear out your summer inventory to make room for fall fashions, you might offer deep discounts to Facebook members who check in with your store using Facebook Places. This chapter shows you how to do that and more with Facebook Places and Deals.

Claiming Your Place

Anyone can add a Facebook Place, and one of your customers may have added a place for your business already. As a business owner, you have the power not only to add a place or claim the place a customer added, but also to customize your Place with a Wall, likes, and more.

> **WHOA!**
>
> To claim your Place, you must prove you're the official representa-
> tive. You need to supply an e-mail address with a domain that clearly
> relates to the business—for example, josiejackson@yourbusiness.com.
> Otherwise, you need to prove ownership when you claim your Place by
> supplying official documentation—in the form of a scanned or photo-
> graphed copy of a utility or phone bill that includes your business name
> and business address.

Check for Your Place

Someone may have already added your Place, saving you the trouble.
To check for your Place, access the Facebook app from your mobile
device or go to touch.facebook.com, and then click the **Places** tab.
Or, if you're using Facebook on a computer, click in the **Search** box
in the top menu and search for your business by name. If your business isn't listed as a Place, you can add it, as explained in the next
section. If your business is listed, you can claim the listing; to do so,
skip ahead to the section titled "Claim Your Place."

Add a Place

If your business isn't listed as a Facebook Place, you can create a place
using the Facebook app on your smartphone or other mobile device.
You should also be able to do this using a computer and web browser
at touch.facebook.com, but during the writing of this book, accessing that URL via computer resulted in very poor functionality, so we
recommend accessing it via your mobile device app or web browser.

To create a place using a smartphone or another mobile communications device that has a browser, follow these steps:

1. Access the Facebook app on your mobile device or use your
   web browser to go to touch.facebook.com, and then click the
   Places tab.

2. Click **Check In**.

3. Click the **Add** button (to the left of the Places Names search
   box, last we checked).

4. Type a name for your Place and a description of it. The default location for your new Place is wherever you're currently located. After claiming your Place, as explained in the next section, you can change the location, if necessary.

5. Click the **Add** button. Facebook prompts you to describe what you're doing at the place and/or tag your friends there.

6. (Optional) Post a description of what you're doing at the place or tag any friends who happen to be there with you.

7. Click the **Check In** button.

Claim Your Place

Assuming your business is already a Facebook Place and you're the rightful owner of said business, you can claim it. When you're ready to claim your business, access its Place page. In the left column, click **Is this your business?**. Click **I certify that I am an official representative of <your business name>**, click **Proceed with Verification**, and complete the Claim Place form. Include as much information on the form as possible, including the business address, phone number, your name and title, and your Federal Employer Identification Number (EIN), if applicable. After completing the form, click **Submit**.

As part of claiming your Place, Facebook verfies ownership via a phone call (by supplying you with a PIN) or by using the documentation you submitted to prove ownership. After you claim your Place and verify ownership, you can manage your Place's business address, contact information, business hours, Profile pictures, administrators, and other settings, and you can merge your Place with your business Page. Head to the next section to find out more about merging your Place and Page.

Merging Your Place and Page

If your business already has a Page, you now have two listings that your customers can interact with. That means two listings you need to monitor and manage. To fix that, merge your Place and Page.

1. Access your Place, as explained earlier, in the section titled "Check for Your Place."

2. Click the **Merge with existing Page** link (the left menu, last we checked). Facebook prompts you to select the Page you want to merge with.

3. Click the Page you want to merge with and click **Merge**. Facebook prompts you to confirm the merge.

4. Click **Confirm**.

After you merge your Place and Page, your Page contains check-in information, and now you're ready to offer customers deals for checking in.

Offering Check-In Deals

Check-in Deals enable your business to present special offers to customers and prospective customers via their Facebook-enabled smartphones or other mobile devices. From a business perspective, Check-in Deals give your business opportunities to generate word-of-mouth advertising, build long-lasting relationships with your customers, attract new customers, and build a community around your brand. Consumers like Check-in Deals, because they can save money engaging in their favorite activities and enrich their experiences by sharing deals with their friends.

Suppose you have a restaurant like Nirvana Grille (www.facebook.com/NirvanaGrille) and you want to increase your dinner crowd by offering a free glass of house wine with every entrée. You can set up a Check-in Deal on Facebook available exclusively to those who "like" your Facebook Page from inside the restaurant. Whenever someone visits your restaurant and checks in to your Place using their smartphone or web-enabled mobile device, they gain instant access to information about the deal, and if they qualify to receive it, they can show it to the server to redeem the offer.

POKE

A Check-in Deal can be a freebie or something Facebook members can purchase, such as six movie tickets for the price of four, or a free dessert at a local restaurant with a qualifying purchase.

Recognizing the Four Types of Check-In Deals

Facebook allows you to create the following four different types of Check-in Deals depending on your goal:

- **Individual Deal:** Individual Deals are great for launching new products, attracting customers, offering seasonal or holiday incentives, and clearing out excess inventory. Both new and existing customers can take advantage of Individual Deals.

- **Friend Deal:** Friend Deals enable you to offer discounts to groups of up to eight people when they check in together. With multiple members checking in and posting stories, Friend Deals increase your exposure on Facebook.

- **Loyalty Deal:** To improve customer retention while generating more business through existing customers, consider offering a Loyalty Deal. The customer receives the deal only after checking in to your Facebook Place a certain number of times (between 2 and 20, according to your preference).

- **Charity Deal:** Charity Deals are excellent for showing your commitment to community. With a Charity Deal, when a customer makes a purchase, you donate a certain amount to the charity of your choice (not the charity of the customer's choice).

WHOA!

At the time of this writing, Check-in Deals was still in Beta and available only to a small number of businesses on Facebook.

Let's Make a Deal

Before creating a deal, make sure everyone in your business who needs to know about the deal is informed. If a customer asks one of your employees about a Check-in Deal on Facebook and your employee claims to have never heard about it, that would be bad. Also, keep in mind that Facebook may take up to 48 hours to review and approve the deal, so plan ahead. If you create a deal that runs tomorrow, tomorrow may pass before your deal gets approved.

Creating a deal is a straightforward process. Here's what you do:

1. Head to your Facebook Page/Place.

2. Click **Edit Page** (upper right).

3. Click **Deals** (left menu).

4. Click **Create a Deal for this Page**. The Create a Deal Page appears, prompting you to enter information about the deal.

5. Click the type of deal you want to create: **Individual, Friend, Loyalty,** or **Charity**.

6. In the Define your offer section, enter a description of the offer, instructions on how to claim it, and any other details; for example, if you're creating a Loyalty Deal, open the **Check-ins required** list and select the number of times the customer must check in to earn the deal.

7. In the Add details and restrictions area, enter additional details about the promotion, including a start and end date and time, and any limitations on quantity or number of claims per customer.

8. Click **Create Deal**. Facebook submits the deal for review, which can take up to 48 hours. After submitting your deal, you'll receive a message providing you with additional instructions on running your deal.

After submitting your deal, review it for accuracy and typos. If you notice any errors, click the **Edit** button and make your changes. To stop the deal at any time, visit your Page/Place, click **Deals** (left menu), click the deal, and click **Stop Deal**. Keep in mind, however, that stopping the deal prematurely and refusing to honor it when customers arrive to claim it is bad business and might even get you into legal trouble (at the very least, customers will "Facebook" about it, and not in a good way).

Promoting Your Check-In Deals

After you've created a Check-in Deal and Facebook has approved it, you can share it via your Page or Place or by creating an ad for it, as explained in Chapter 18. One of the best, easiest, and cheapest (free) ways to share a deal is to post it as a status update on your Page/ Place. This spreads the word to all the folks who "like" or visit your Page/Place. Even without posting an ad, you, Facebook, and your fans can team up to spread the word about your deal organically; here's how:

- **Check-in Deals page:** By visiting www.facebook.com/deals/ checkin, Facebook members can see all the Check-in Deals in their home zip code.

- **Smartphone:** When a Facebook member clicks **Places** on the smartphone's Facebook app, the app orients the phone to current geographical location, and any Check-in Deals in the local area appear.

- **Messages, Wall posts, and News Feed updates:** Members may share your Check-in Deal with their friends by posting an update about it or messaging their friends. As members access your Check-in Deal, their interactions show up in their News Feed, sharing the information about your offer with their friends.

- **Deals Tab:** When users select the **Deals** tab in the Facebook app for their mobile device, your deal is eligible to appear on the right side of any deal currently running on the page.

Offering Other Deals on Facebook

In the spring of 2011, Facebook began promoting another type of deal for businesses to offer their fans and others looking for discounts. Facebook Deals or Daily Deals, which is different from Facebook Check-in Deals, are similar offerings to those you see from popular daily deal websites such as Groupon.com, LivingSocial.com, and BuyWithMe.com. Using Facebook Deals, your business can market Daily Deals, discounted gift certificates, and group coupons to Facebook members on either a local or national level.

At the time of this writing, Facebook Deals was only available in five local U.S. markets: Atlanta, Austin, Dallas, San Diego, and San Francisco. To learn more about offering deals to Facebook members in your market, visit www.facebook.com/deals/business and click the **Contact Us** link to tell Facebook you're ready to get started whenever they are.

The Least You Need to Know

- If your business isn't listed as a Facebook Place, use your smartphone or web-enabled device to add it.
- Once your Place is on Facebook, claim it, so you can manage it.
- To claim your Place, head to the place, click **Is this your business?**, and follow the on-screen cues to complete the process.
- To create a Check-in Deal, head to your Facebook Page, click **Edit Page**, click **Deals** (left menu), and follow the on-screen cues to complete the process.
- After creating a deal, post a status update on your Page/Place to start spreading the word, and make sure your staff is in the loop on the details of the offer.
- For more about Facebook Deals (different from Facebook Check-in Deals), visit www.facebook.com/deals/business to learn more.

Glossary

ad   Short for *advertisement*, a paid promotion on Facebook that typically consists of an image, a small chunk of text, and a link, often displayed in the right column of most Facebook Pages.

admin   Short for *administrator*, a Facebook member who has greater access and authority to manage and configure a group, Page, or other user-generated area on Facebook.

API   Short for *application programming interface*, a set of programming instructions, procedures, and protocols accessible via the Internet that support the building of applications on Facebook and other platforms.

app   Short for *application*, a Facebook plugin that adds functionality to Facebook, such as enabling users to upload photos or videos and play games.

Chat   A Facebook tool that enables friends to exchange text messages in real time.

Check-in Deal   A Facebook product that enables businesses to create geolocation-based deals on Facebook, which members can access and redeem by checking in to a business's Facebook Place using their smartphone.

comment   A remark posted in response to an existing status update or other content, such as a note, photo, or video.

Deals   A Facebook feature that enables businesses to present special offers, discounted gift certificates, and group coupons to Facebook members.

developer   Someone with programming skills who develops apps on Facebook.

Event A Facebook app that enables you to announce special occasions or gatherings, invite Facebook users to attend, and keep everyone you invited posted about any developments related to the happening.

Facebook An online social network that enables friends, family members, colleagues, classmates, acquaintances, businesses, brands, and organizations to get in touch and stay in touch and meet others who may share their interests or experiences.

fan A term used to describe someone who "likes" a Facebook Page.

feed A connection that pulls content from another source on the Internet and displays it on Facebook.

footer The area at the bottom of every Facebook Page containing links to About Facebook, Advertising, Create a Page, Careers, Terms, Help, and other offerings.

friend list A subset of friends that provides you with an easier way to follow and communicate exclusively with that set of friends. Think of it as a clique.

friend request A standardized message sent to another Facebook member whom you want to friend on Facebook.

friends Any two people who mutually agree to connect with one another on Facebook.

friendship page An area that contains the public Wall posts and comments between two friends, photos in which they're both tagged, events they've both RSVP'd, and more. You can view a friendship page if you're friends with at least one of the members and have permission to view both members' Profiles.

Gift A Facebook app that allows friends to exchange digital presents, which can sometimes be exchanged for real presents outside of Facebook.

Group An area on Facebook where users with shared interests can gather. Groups can be exclusive or open to all.

Insights A tool that provides developers and businesses with metrics regarding their content and the Facebook members who interact with it. Insights provide valuable data for analysis of user growth, demographics, and user-content interaction.

left menu   The menu bar that runs along the left side of most Facebook Pages and enables you to access the most frequently used Facebook features.

Like   A link you can click to indicate positive sentiment for something one of your friends or some other Facebook member has posted.

member   Anyone with a Facebook account.

Messages   A Facebook feature that enables members to communicate with one another more privately. Messages between friends include actual messages, Facebook chatting, and any Facebook e-mail they exchange.

Mobile   A Facebook app that enables you to log in to your Facebook account and use Facebook from a cell phone or other portable communications device.

network   An offline community of people related by locale or experience, such as a town, school, or place of employment.

News Feed   One of the main areas on Facebook, which displays activities your friends have chosen to share with you.

Notes   A core Facebook app that enables you to post longer entries than you'd normally post in a status update and provides a way to feed your blog (if you have one) into your Facebook Profile.

notification   A message Facebook sends you and/or displays on the notification list to let you know when something of importance has occurred, such as someone commenting on your status update or the receipt of a message.

officer   A Facebook user in a group who holds a special status but doesn't have the privileges to configure or manage the group as an admin. *See* admin.

Page   A Facebook feature that's typically used to promote a business, organization, product, or brand.

Photos   A core Facebook app that enables you to upload digital photographs to your account and create, manage, and share photo galleries.

Places   A Facebook feature that enables members to share where they are, connect with friends nearby, and find special deals based on their current location. Businesses use Places to offer discounts and other specials.

Poke   A Facebook feature that enables you to let a friend know, in real time, that you're thinking about him or her.

Profile   A collection of information a Facebook member enters about herself along with an optional photo.

Publisher   The tool for posting Facebook status updates to a Wall or the News Feed.

RSS feed   *See* feed.

SMS   Acronym for *Short Message Service*, a technology that enables the exchange of text messages using a cell phone or other mobile communications device. Through the magic of SMS, you can also post content to Facebook using a mobile phone.

status update   A microblogging tool on Facebook that enables members to post brief messages, typically to share observations, insights, and experiences.

tag   To label yourself or a friend in a photo, video, note, or other item posted on Facebook. When you tag someone else, Facebook sends the person a notification.

top menu   The blue bar at the top of every Facebook Page that enables you to access the most frequently used areas on Facebook.

Video   A core Facebook app that enables users to upload and share video clips.

Wall   A quieter area on Facebook where you and your friends can post status updates, comments, photos, video clips, links, and more. While the News Feed displays all activity, the Wall filters out a lot of stuff to focus more on your recent activity and what you and your friends specifically post on one another's Walls.

Index

A

accessing
  Events application, 158
  Facebook on smartphones, 202
  messages, 88
  Notes application, 170-172
  personal Profile, 39-40
  Video page, 122
accessorizing Pages, 238
Account button, 13
Account Settings page, 82
accounts
  deactivation, 20-21
  deletion, 21
  settings, 15-17
activities, 4-5
Add Featured Likes setting
  (Pages), 235
address book (e-mail), 6
administrators (groups), 137
Admins option (Pages), 235
Adobe Flash Player Settings
  dialog box, 124
Ads (Facebook Ads), 245
  benefits, 246-247
  calls to action, 250-251
  drawbacks, 247
  effective messages, 251
  images, 251-252
  launching ad campaign, 252
    creating ad, 252-253
    monitoring campaign,
      256-257
    pricing/scheduling
      preferences, 254-255
    reviewing/approving ads,
      255
    targeting demographic,
      253-254
  listing keywords, 250
  measurable goals, 249-250
  rules and regulations, 248-249
  targeting a demographic/
    locale, 250
advertisement opportunities, 219
  cross-promotion on blog/
    website, 220
  Facebook for Websites,
    221-222
  Facebook Places/Deals, 222
  launching a Facebook Page,
    219-220
  posting ads, 221
advertisements. *See* Ads

albums (photos), 105
  editing, 107
    customizing individual
      photos, 108-109
    rearranging photos, 111
    tagging photos, 109-111
  management with third-party
    applications, 112
    Flickr, 114-116
    Picasa, 113-114
Android operating system, 202
Apple App Store, 202
applications, 15
  authorizing, 184-186
  Chat, 144
    going on/offline, 146-147
    setting options, 150-155
    viewing and deleting history,
      145
  editing/removing, 189-190
  Events
    accessing, 158
    creating events, 162-166
    scheduled events, 158-162
  Notes, 169
    accessing, 170-172
    blog posts, 176-177
    posting notes, 173-175
    reviewing notes, 175
    tagging notes, 175-176
  privacy settings, 28-31
  responding to/sending
    requests, 187-188
  searching/browsing, 182-184
  smartphones (Facebook
    Mobile), 202
    Facebook Deals, 211-213
    Facebook Mobile Web, 208
    Facebook Places, 209-211
    setting up, 202-204
    status updates, 205
    texting commands, 205-206
    texting to, 204
    uploading photos/videos,
      207-208
approvals
  ads (Facebook Ads), 255
  responding to posts, 78
Apps Directory link, 115, 183
archiving messages, 93
attachments
  photos, 74-75
  video, 76
authorizing applications, 184-186

B

Basic Information, 46
Bejeweled Blitz, 193
BlackBerry's app store, 202
blocking individuals, 31-32
blogs
  feeding to business Page,
    238-239
  posts, 176-177
browsing
  applications, 182-184
  events, 160-161
Budget category (Facebook Ads),
  254
businesses, 217-218
  advertisement opportunities,
    219
    cross-promotion on blog/
      website, 220
    Facebook for Websites,
      221-222
    Facebook Places/Deals, 222
    launching a Facebook Page,
      219-220
    posting ads, 221

engaging members with
Facebook applications,
223-224

etiquette, 224-226

Facebook Ads, 245

benefits, 246-247

calls to action, 250-251

drawbacks, 247

effective messages, 251

images, 251-252

launching ad campaign,
252-257

listing keywords, 250

measurable goals, 249-250

rules and regulations,
248-249

targeting a demographic/
locale, 250

Facebook Deals, 262

creating a deal, 263-264

Daily Deals, 265-266

promoting deal, 264-265

Facebook Places

adding a Place, 260-261

checking for your Place,
260

claiming Place, 259-261

merging Place and Page,
261-262

groups, 222-223

Pages, 227

accessorizing with third-
party applications, 238

adding content, 236-237

adjusting Page settings,
233-235

building/maintaining fan
base, 240-241

creating, 230-232

customizing, 228-230

expanding content, 238

feeding blog to business
Page, 238-239

hiding/deleting Pages, 236

home page, 232

tracking Insights, 241-242

buttons

Account, 13

Check In, 210

Complete Sign-Up, 10

Confirm, 21

Create Doc, 140

Edit My Profile, 14

Edit Profile, 39

Edit Settings, 189

Edit Thumbnail, 43

Find Friends, 13

Home, 13

Message Guests, 165

Poke, 82

Preview My Profile, 27

Profile, 13

Review Ad, 255

Save & Continue, 8

Share Deal, 213

Sign Up, 6

Start Importing, 176

Stop Importing, 177

Take a Photo, 9

Upload a Photo, 9

C

Café World, 193

calls to action (Facebook Ads),
250-251

Campaign & Budget category
(Facebook Ads), 254

campaigns (Facebook Ads),
254-255

changing Profile pictures, 40
  clipping thumbnail, 44
  hiding/unhiding photos in
    Photostream, 45
  picture selection, 44
  uploading digital photos, 41-42
  webcam photos, 42-43
Charity Deals, 212, 263
Chat application, 15, 88, 144
  going on/offline, 146-147
  groups, 139
  setting options, 150
    Friend Lists feature, 153-155
    Online Friends Window,
      152-153
    pop-out chat window, 151
    sound for new messages,
      152
  viewing and deleting history,
    145
Check In button, 210
Check-in Deals, 211-213, 262
  creating a deal, 263-264
  promoting deal, 264-265
CityVille, 192
clipping thumbnails, 44
closed groups, 130
Code of Conduct, 122
collaboration, group documents,
  140
commands, 205-206
comments
  notes, 172
  responding to posts, 78
  video clips, 119
communication
  Messages feature, 87
    accessing, 88
    adding someone to
      conversation, 90

archiving/deleting messages,
  93
e-mail, 88
flagging unread messages,
  92
forwarding messages, 91
leaving the conversation, 91
notifications, 96-97
online chatting, 88
reading/replying, 89-90
reporting spam, 93
searching for messages,
  91-92
sending messages, 93-95
text messaging, 88
Wall, 70
  attachments, 74-77
  bumping into a friends wall,
    71
  heading to, 70-71
  inserting links, 76-77
  liking and sharing stuff,
    83-84
  posting to, 72-74, 80-83
  responding to posts, 77-80
Complete Sign-Up button, 10
completing sign up, 10
computer uploads, video, 123
Confirm button, 21
Connecting on Facebook (privacy
  page), 25-26
connecting to friends, 51
contact information, editing, 49
Contact Us link, 266
content, Pages, 236-238
conversations
  adding someone to, 90
  groups, 133-135
  leaving, 91
core features, 14

cost per thousand impressions (CPM), 247

cost-per-click (CPC) advertising, 246

CPC (cost-per-click) advertising, 246

CPM (cost per thousand impressions), 247

Create an Album option, 75

Create Doc button, 140

creating
deals (Check-In Deals), 263-264
events, 162-166
groups, 135
adding friends, 137
administrators, 137
e-mail address, 136
removal of members, 137-138
Pages, 230-232

cross-promotion, Facebook and blog/website, 220

Custom Privacy dialog box, 26

Customize settings link, 211

Customize Settings page, 28

customizing
Pages, 228-230
photos, 108-109

D

Daily Deals, 212, 265-266

deactivation of account, 20-21

Deals (Facebook Deals), 222, 262
Charity Deals, 263
Check-in Deals, 211-213
creating a deal, 263-264
Daily Deals, 265-266
Friend Deals, 263

Individual Deals, 263
Loyalty Deals, 263
promoting deal, 264-265

Deals tab, 265

deleting
accounts, 21
Chat history, 145
messages, 93
Pages, 236

demographics (Facebook Ads), 250

digital video formats, 123

documents, groups, 140

downloading photos, 104

E

e-mail
address book, 6
communication, 88
creating group address, 136
sending video messages, 127-128

Edit Ad link, 255

Edit My Profile, 39
changing Profile picture, 40-41
editing information, 46
basic information, 46
contact information, 49
education and work, 48
Featured People, 47
personal information, 48
picture selection, 44-45
uploading digital photos, 41-42
webcam photos, 42-43

Edit My Profile button, 14

Edit Profile button, 39

Edit Settings button, 189

Edit Settings link, 203

Edit Thumbnail button, 43
Edit Your News Feed Settings
  dialog box, 79
editing
  applications, 189-190
  photos, 103
    customizing individual
      photos, 108-109
    rearranging photos, 111
    tagging photos, 109-111
  Profile, 39
    basic information, 46
    contact information, 49
    education and work, 48
    Featured People, 47
    personal information, 48
  videos, 125-126
education, 48
Email Notifications option
  (Pages), 233
embedding videos, 126-127
etiquette, 17-19, 224-226
Eventbrite, 238
events
  creating, 162-166
  groups, 138-139
  scheduled, 158
    poking for events, 159-160
    RSVP-ing, 161-162
    searching/browsing, 160-161
Events application
  accessing, 158
  creating events, 162-166
  scheduled events, 158
    poking for events, 159-160
    RSVP-ing, 161-162
    searching/browsing, 160-161
Events option (News Feed), 69
expanding Page content, 238
exploring groups, 132-133

F

Facebook Ads tab, 17
Facebook Deals, 222, 262-263
  Check-in Deals, 211-213
  creating a deal, 263-264
  Daily Deals, 265-266
  promoting deal, 264-265
Facebook for Websites, 221-222
Facebook icon, 12
Facebook Mobile Web, 208
Facebook Places, 209, 222
  adding a Place, 260-261
  checking for your Place, 260
  checking in, 210
  claiming Place, 259-261
  merging Place and Page,
    261-262
  privacy settings, 211
  starting, 210
fan base, business Page, 240-241
FarmVille, 192
Featured People, 47
Find Friends button, 13
finding
  friends, 6
  games, 194-195
flagging unread messages, 92
Flash Player, 118
Flickr photo management, 114-116
folders, photos, 104
forwarding messages, 91
Friend Deals, 212, 263
Friend Lists feature (chat),
  153-155
Friend Requests icon, 12
friends
  connecting to, 51
  creating groups, 137
  finding, 6

Friends option (News Feed), 69
FrontierVille, 192

G

games, 15, 191
  Bejeweled Blitz, 193
  Café World, 193
  CityVille, 192
  FarmVille, 192
  finding, 194-195
  FrontierVille, 192
  inviting friends, 197-198
  launching, 196
  Mafia Wars, 193
  making friends, 198
  Pet Society, 193
  Ravenwood Fair, 193
  requests, 187
  responding to requests, 198
  Texas Hold'Em Poker, 192
  Treasure Isle, 194
Games Directory link, 195
goals, Facebook Ads, 249-250
groups, 129-130
  businesses, 222-223
  chatting, 139
  closed, 130
  collaboration on documents,
    140
  conversations, 133-135
  creating, 135
    adding friends, 137
    administrators, 137
    e-mail address, 136
    removal of members,
      137-138
  creating events, 138-139
  exploring, 132-133

  finding through friends,
    131-132
  joining, 133
  leaving, 133
  open, 130
  searching for, 130-131
  secret, 130
  sharing photos, 138
guidelines, uploading video clips,
  121-122

H

hackers, protection strategies,
  32-35
heading to Wall, 70-71
Help system, 19-20
hiding
  Pages, 236
  Photostream photos, 45
  status updates, 79-80
  updates, 79-80
Home button, 13
Home page, 232
HTML tags, 174

I

images (Facebook Ads), 251-252
Importr (Flickr), 115
Individual Deals, 212, 263
inserting links, 76-77
Insights (Pages), 235, 241-242
instant personalization, 31
interactive blogging, 170
interface, 11
  account settings, 15-17
  left menu, 14-15
  News Feed, 14

Publisher, 14
right column, 15
top menu, 12-13
invitations
games, 197-198
groups, 132

links
inserting, 76-77
notes, 172
locating friends, 6
logging in/out, 11
Loyalty Deals, 212, 263

J-K

joining groups, 133

keywords (Facebook Ads), 250
kids and Facebook, protection
strategies, 36-37

L

Language tab, 16
launching
advertisement campaigns, 252
creating ad, 252-253
monitoring campaigns,
256-257
pricing/scheduling
preferences, 254-255
reviewing/approving ads,
255
targeting demographic,
253-254
Facebook Page, 219-220
games, 196
layout (Pages), 229-230
leaving
conversations, 91
groups, 133
left menu, 14-15
Like link, 78
liking stuff, 83-84

M

Mafia Wars, 193
Manage Permissions option
(Pages), 234
management, photos, 112-116
mass mailing messages, 95
measurable goals (Facebook Ads),
249-250
menus
left, 14-15
top, 12-13
Message Guests button, 165
messages
Facebook Ads, 251
video e-mail, 127-128
Messages feature, 87
accessing, 88
adding someone to
conversation, 90
archiving/deleting messages,
93
e-mail, 88
flagging unread messages, 92
forwarding messages, 91
leaving the conversation, 91
notifications, 96-97
online chatting, 88
reading/replying, 89-90
reporting spam, 93
searching for messages, 91-92

sending messages, 93
  Facebook members, 94-95
  mass mailing, 95
  non-Facebook members, 95
  text messaging, 88
Messages icon, 12
Messages option (News Feed), 69
microblogging, 72
Mobile Facebook
  setting up, 202-204
  status updates, 205
  texting Facebook commands, 205-206
  texting to, 204
  uploading photos/videos, 207-208
  Web, 208
Mobile tab, 16
monitoring ad campaigns (Facebook Ads), 256-257
Most Recent option (News Feed), 69

N

Networks tab, 16
News Feed, 14, 68-70
  liking and sharing stuff, 83-84
  posting to, 72
    attachments, 77
    friends' walls, 80-83
    inserting a link, 76-77
    photo attachments, 74-75
    questions, 73-74
    video attachments, 76
  responding to posts, 77
    comments, 78
    hiding updates, 79-80
    voting approvals, 78

Notes application, 169
  accessing, 170-172
  blog posts, 176-177
  posting notes, 173-175
  reviewing notes, 175
  tagging notes, 175-176
notifications, 96-97
Notifications icon, 13, 16

O

offline (Chat status), 146-147
Old Reliable menu (top menu), 12-13
one-on-one communication. *See* Messages feature
online chatting, 88, 146-147
Online Friends Window (chat), 152-153
open groups, 130
organizing photos, 104

P

Pages (businesses), 227
  accessorizing with third-party applications, 238
  adding content, 236-237
  adjusting Page settings, 233-235
  building/maintaining fan base, 240-241
  creating, 230-232
  customizing, 228-230
  expanding content, 238
  feeding blog to business Page, 238-239
  hiding/deleting, 236
  Home page, 232

merging with Place, 261-262
tracking Insights, 241-242
paired HTML tags, 174
pay-per-click advertising, 249
pay-per-view advertising, 250
Payments tab, 16
personal Profile
    accessing, 39-40
    changing your photo, 40-41
    editing information, 46
        basic information, 46
        contact information, 49
        education and work, 48
        Featured People, 47
        personal information, 48
    picture selection, 44-45
    uploading digital photos, 41-42
    webcam photos, 42-43
Pet Society, 193
phishers, protection strategies, 32-35
photos
    attachments, 74-75
    changing Profile pictures, 40-41
    management with third-party applications, 112
        Flickr, 114-116
        Picasa, 113-114
    picture selection, 44-45
    sharing with groups, 138
    uploading, 101
        albums, 105-107
        customizing individual photos, 108-109
        editing photos, 103, 107-108
        Facebook Mobile, 207-208
        organizing photos, 104
        Profile pictures, 8-9

rearranging photos, 111
tagging photos, 109-111
uploading digital photos, 41-42
webcam photos, 42-43
Photostream, 45, 102
Picasa, 113-114
Places (Facebook Places), 209, 222
    adding a Place, 260-261
    checking for your Place, 260
    checking in, 210
    claiming Place, 259-261
    merging Place and Page, 261-262
    privacy settings, 211
    starting, 210
Poke button, 82
poking a friend, 82
Polls (Pages), 238
pop-out chat window, 151
posting
    ads to Facebook, 221
    notes, 173-175
    status updates, 205
    Wall/News Feed, 72
        attachments, 77
        friends' walls, 80-83
        hiding updates, 79-80
        inserting a link, 76-77
        liking and sharing stuff, 83-84
        photo attachments, 74-75
        questions, 73-74
        responding to posts, 77-78
        video attachments, 76
Posting Preferences option (Pages), 233
Preview My Profile button, 27
pricing Facebook Ads, 254-255
Pricing category (Facebook Ads), 255

privacy settings, 23
  applications and websites, 28-31
  blocking individuals, 31-32
  Connecting on Facebook, 25-26
  Facebook Places, 211
  protection strategies, 32-34
    kids and Facebook, 36-37
    reporting scams, 36
    spam, 35
  sharing on Facebook, 26-28
Profile, 39
  accessing, 39-40
  changing your photo, 40-41
  editing information, 46
    basic information, 46
    contact information, 49
    education and work, 48
    Featured People, 47
    personal information, 48
  picture selection, 44-45
  uploading digital photos, 41-42
  webcam photos, 42-43
Profile button, 13
Profile pictures, 8-9
promotional opportunities
  advertisement opportunities, 219
    cross-promotion on blog/website, 220
    Facebook for Websites, 221-222
    Facebook Places/Deals, 222
    launching a Facebook Page, 219-220
    posting ads, 221
  deals (Check-in Deals), 264-265

  engaging members with Facebook applications, 223-224
  etiquette, 224-226
Facebook Ads, 245
  benefits, 246-247
  calls to action, 250-251
  drawbacks, 247
  effective messages, 251
  images, 251-252
  launching ad campaigns, 252-257
  listing keywords, 250
  measurable goals, 249-250
  rules and regulations, 248-249
  targeting a demographic/locale, 250
Facebook Deals, 262
  creating a deal, 263-264
  Daily Deals, 265-266
  promoting deal, 264-265
Facebook Places
  adding a Place, 260-261
  checking for your Place, 260
  claiming Place, 259-261
  merging Place and Page, 261-262
groups, 222-223
Pages, 227
  accessorizing with third-party applications, 238
  adding content, 236-237
  adjusting Page settings, 233-235
  building/maintaining fan base, 240-241
  creating, 230-232
  customizing, 228-230

expanding content, 238
feeding blog to business
 Page, 238-239
hiding/deleting, 236
Home page, 232
tracking Insights, 241-242
protection strategies, 32
 kids and Facebook, 36-37
 reporting scams, 36
 spam, 35
Publisher, 14

Q-R

quitting Facebook, 20-21

Ravenwood Fair, 193
reading messages, 89-90
Really Simple Syndication (RSS)
 feeds, 97
rearranging photos, 111
Record a Video option, 76
recording video clips, 121
registration, 5
 completing sign up, 10
 finding friends, 6
 logging in/out, 11
 Profile pictures, 8-9
 workplace and school
  information, 7-8
regulations, 17-18, 248-249
relationship status, 47
removal
 applications, 189-190
 group members, 137-138
replying to messages, 89-90
reporting
 scams, 36
 spam, 93

Request for Permission box, 187
responding to
 application requests, 187-188
 game requests, 198
 posts, 77
  comments, 78
  hiding updates, 79-80
  voting approvals, 78
return on investment (ROI), 242
Review Ad button, 255
reviewing
 ads (Facebook Ads), 255
 notes, 175
Reviews (Pages), 238
right column, 15
ROI (return on investment), 242
RSS (Really Simple Syndication)
 feeds, 97
RSVP-ing to events, 161-162
rules, 17-18, 248-249

S

Save & Continue button, 8
scams, 36
Schedule category (Facebook
 Ads), 254
scheduled events, 158
 poking for events, 159-160
 RSVP-ing, 161-162
 searching/browsing, 160-161
scheduling (Facebook Ads),
 254-255
school information, 7-8
Search box, 13
search engine optimization
 (SEO), 250
searching
 applications, 182-184
 events, 160-161

groups, 130-132
messages, 91-92
secret groups, 130
security applications, 186
See Friendship link, 80
sending
  application requests, 187-188
  messages, 93
    Facebook members, 94-95
    mass mailing, 95
    non-Facebook members, 95
SEO (search engine optimization), 250
settings
  accounts, 15-17
  Chat options, 150
    Friend Lists feature, 153-155
    Online Friends Window, 152-153
    pop-out chat window, 151
    sound for new messages, 152
  Pages, 233-235
  privacy, 23
    applications and websites, 28-31
    blocking individuals, 31-32
    Connecting on Facebook, 25-26
    protection strategies, 32-37
    sharing on Facebook, 26-28
Settings tab, 16
Share Deal button, 213
Share link, 78
sharing, 26-28
  Deals (Facebook Deals), 213
  notes, 172
  photos, 101
    albums, 105-107
    customizing individual photos, 108-109

editing photos, 103, 107-108
groups, 138
management with third-party applications, 112-116
organizing photos, 104
rearranging photos, 111
tagging photos, 109-111
videos, 117
  accessing Video page, 122
  commenting on clips, 119
  computer uploads, 123
  editing videos, 125-126
  embedding videos, 126-127
  guidelines, 121-122
  recording footage, 121
  sending via e-mail, 127-128
  tagging clips, 119-120
  watching a clip, 118-121
  webcam recordings, 124-125
Sign Up button, 6
signing up on Facebook, 5
  completing sign up, 10
  finding friends, 6
  logging in/out, 11
  Profile pictures, 8-9
  workplace and school information, 7-8
smartphones, 202
  Facebook Deals, 211-213
  Facebook Mobile Web, 202-204, 208
  Facebook Places, 209-211
  status updates, 205
  texting Facebook commands, 205-206
  texting to Facebook, 204
  uploading photos/videos, 207-208
social games, 191
  Bejeweled Blitz, 193
  Café World, 193

CityVille, 192
FarmVille, 192
finding, 194-195
FrontierVille, 192
inviting friends, 197-198
launching, 196
Mafia Wars, 193
making friends, 198
Pet Society, 193
Ravenwood Fair, 193
responding to requests, 198
Texas Hold'Em Poker, 192
Treasure Isle, 194
social networking, 3-5
sound, chat messages, 152
spam
    protection strategies, 35
    reporting, 93
Start Importing button, 176
status updates
    Facebook Mobile, 205
    hiding, 79-80
Stop Importing button, 177
strategies, protection, 32-34
    kids and Facebook, 36-37
    reporting scams, 36
    spam, 35

T

tagging
    notes, 175-176
    photos, 109-111
    video clips, 119-120
Take a Photo button, 9
Take a Profile Picture dialog box, 42
targeting demographic/locale (Facebook Ads), 250

Terms of Service, 17
Terms of Use, 122
Testimonials (Pages), 238
text messaging, 88, 204-206
third-party applications
    accessorizing Pages, 238
    photo management, 112
        Flickr, 114-116
        Picasa, 113-114
threats, protection strategies, 32-34
    kids and Facebook, 36-37
    reporting scams, 36
    spam, 35
thumbnails, clipping, 44
top menu, 12-13
Top News option (News Feed), 69
tracking Page Insights, 241-242
Treasure Isle, 194

U

unhiding, Photostream photos, 45
unpaired HTML tags, 174
unread messages, 92
Unsubscribe link, 135
unsubscribing from groups, 135
updates, hiding, 79-80
Upload a Photo button, 9
Upload a Video option, 76
uploading
    photos, 74-75, 101
        albums, 105-107
        customizing individual photos, 108-109
        editing photos, 103, 107-108
        Facebook Mobile, 207-208

management with third-party applications, 112-116

organizing photos, 104

Profile pictures, 8-9, 40-42

rearranging photos, 111

tagging photos, 109-111

videos, 117

accessing Video page, 122

commenting on clips, 119

computer uploads, 123

guidelines, 121-122

recording footage, 121

tagging clips, 119-120

watching a clip, 118-121

webcam recordings, 124-125

V

vanity URLs, 225

Video page, 122

videos

attachments, 76

editing, 125-126

embedding, 126-127

sending via e-mail, 127-128

uploading and sharing, 117

accessing Video page, 122

commenting on clips, 119

computer uploads, 123

Facebook Mobile, 207-208

guidelines, 121-122

recording footage, 121

tagging clips, 119-120

watching a clip, 118-121

webcam recordings, 124-125

View Admins link, 137

View Full Note link, 171

View Original Post link, 172

viewing Chat history, 145

voting approvals, 78

W-X-Y-Z

Wall, 70

bumping into a friend's wall, 71-72

heading to, 70-71

liking and sharing stuff, 83-84

posting to, 72

attachments, 77

friends' walls, 80-83

inserting a link, 76-77

photo attachments, 74-75

questions, 73-74

video attachments, 76

responding to posts, 77

comments, 78

hiding updates, 79-80

voting approvals, 78

watching video clips, 118-121

Web, Facebook Mobile, 208

webcam photos, 42-43

webcam recordings, 124-125

websites

Facebook for Websites, 221-222

privacy settings, 28-31

Welcome option (News Feed), 68

workplace information, 7-8, 48

CHECK OUT THESE
BEST-SELLERS

More than 450 titles available at booksellers and online retailers everywhere!

Grammar and Style
SECOND EDITION
978-1-59257-115-4

Word Search Puzzles
978-1-59257-900-6

Glycemic Index Weight Loss
SECOND EDITION
978-1-59257-855-9

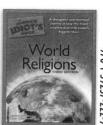
World Religions
THIRD EDITION
978-1-59257-222-9

U.S. HISTORY
GRAPHIC ILLUSTRATED
978-1-59257-785-9

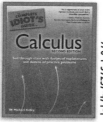
Calculus
SECOND EDITION
978-1-59257-471-1

Positive Dog Training
SECOND EDITION
978-1-59257-483-4

Personal Finance in Your 20s & 30s
FOURTH EDITION
978-1-59257-883-2

CD INCLUDED!

Learning Spanish
FIFTH EDITION
978-1-59257-908-2

Wine Basics
SECOND EDITION
978-1-59257-786-6

Microsoft Windows 7
978-1-59257-954-9

CD INCLUDED!

Music Theory
SECOND EDITION
978-1-59257-437-7

The Perfect Resume
FIFTH EDITION
978-1-59257-957-0

Organizing Your Life
FIFTH EDITION
978-1-59257-966-2

Walt Disney World
978-1-59257-888-7

ALPHA   idiotsguides.com

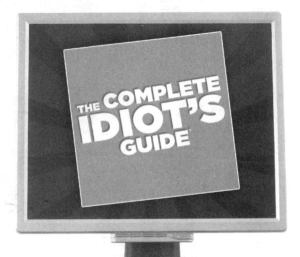